Becoming a

Critical thinker

SECOND EDITION

VINCENT RYAN RUGGIERO

Printed in the U.S.A.

Library of Congress Catalog Card Number: 95-79476

ISBN: 0-395-77250-8

123456789-B-99 98 97 96 95

Second edition

Notice: *Becoming a Critical Thinker* was previously
titled *Critical Thinking*

    COLLEGE SURVIVAL
    A Program of Houghton Mifflin Company
    P.O. Box 8306
    Rapid City, SD 57709-8306

As part of Houghton Mifflin's ongoing commitment to the environment,
this text has been printed on recycled paper.

Acknowledgments

MANY PEOPLE CONTRIBUTED to the second edition of this book. I thank Doug Toft for his editing of the manuscript. Also helpful in proofreading and indexing were Ellen Whalen and Bernice Eisen.

The layout and design of any book contribute greatly to its readability. I appreciate the masterful design work of Amherst & Reeves's Jeff Swaim and the assistance he received from Kim Oslund in production. For their contribution to the illustrations and photography, I thank John Backlund, Mike Wolforth, Doug Garcia, Susan Turnbull, and Gail Chase.

I am especially grateful for the support and insights of Alison Zetterquist and Bill Webber, my editors at Houghton Mifflin, and of Dave Ellis, author of *Becoming a Master Student* and publisher of the first edition of this book.

Request

I am interested in how this book has worked for you. Please write and share your experience.

If you have an idea for improving the book, I will be pleased to receive it. Thank you.

Vincent Ryan Ruggiero
P.O. Box 1155
Dunedin, FL 34697

Table of Contents

Chapter 1 Mastering the Fundamentals

What is thinking? 2
Critical thinking is crucial . . .4
What is truth? 6
A helpful principle 9
Recognize opinions 10
Test opinions 14
Evaluate evidence 18
Dare to change your mind   20
A sample issue 21
A comprehensive thinking
   strategy 22
   Step 1: Observe 22
   Step 2: Record your
      observations 24
   Step 3: Address relevant
      questions 25
Quiz 31

Chapter 2 Becoming an Individual

Understanding individuality   34
Knowing your attitudes
   and values 36
Knowing your mental
   habits 40
Some characteristics of
   critical thinkers 45
   Critical thinkers are honest
      with themselves 45
   Critical thinkers resist
      manipulation 46
   Critical thinkers overcome
      confusion 46

Critical thinkers ask
   questions 47
Critical thinkers take
   the time to produce
   many ideas 47
Critical thinkers base their
   judgments on evidence 48
Critical thinkers acknowledge
   complexity 48
Critical thinkers look for
   connections between
   subjects 49
Critical thinkers are
   intellectually
   independent 49
Quiz 57–58

Chapter 3 Evaluating Longer Arguments

What is an argument? 60
   Step 1: Understand the
      argument 62
      Skim for the main idea .62
      Read with the main
         idea in mind 62
      Identify evidence 62
      Summarize 63
   Step 2: Seek out competing
      views and additional
      evidence 68
   Step 3: Sort out
      disagreements 70
   Step 4: Test the argument
      for reasonableness 72
      Testing evidence 72
      Testing opinions 73
Quiz 79–80

Chapter 4
Recognizing Errors in Thinking

Three kinds of errors 82
  Errors of perception 83
    "Mine is better" thinking 83
    Selective perception . . .84
    Gullibility and skepticism 84
    Bias toward the majority
      or the minority 84
    Pretending to know . . .84
    Bias for or against change 85
    Either/or thinking 85
  Errors of judgment 87
    Double standard 87
    Irrelevant criterion 87
    Overgeneralizing or
      stereotyping 88
    Hasty conclusion 88
    Unwarranted assumption 88
    Failure to make a
      distinction 89
    Oversimplification 89
  Errors of reaction 92
    Explaining away 92
    Shifting the burden of
      proof 93
    Attacking the person . . .93
    Straw man 93
  Errors can multiply 95
Quiz 98–100

Chapter 5 Applying Critical Thinking

Thinking critically about
  commercials 102
    Bandwagon 102
    Glittering generality   102
    Empty comparison . . .103
    Meaningless slogan . . .103
    Testimonial 103
    Transfer 103
Thinking critically about
  print advertising 106
Thinking critically about
  television programming 108
Thinking critically about
  music 114
Thinking critically about
  magazines 116
Thinking critically about
  newspapers 118
Expressing your ideas
  persuasively 120
  Guideline 1: Complete the
    thinking process first   120
  Guideline 2: Use your
    viewpoint as your
    controlling idea 121
  Guideline 3: Choose a
    suitable organization   121
  Guideline 4: Support your
    view with evidence . . .121

  Guideline 5: Be exact
    but lively 122
  Guideline 6: Vary your
    paragraph length 122
  Guideline 7: Proofread your
    composition for acceptable
    punctuation, grammar,
    and usage 122
Quiz 123–124

Epilogue Make the End
  a Beginning 125

Bibliography 126–127

Index 128–129

About the Author 130

Quiz Answers . .131–134

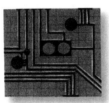

About this book

This book includes numerous opportunities to develop your thinking skills and apply them to real-life situations. These opportunities are of two kinds:

EXERCISES

These assignments are indicated by a *question mark*. They invite you to examine ideas, draw conclusions, and do related tasks, such as writing an explanation of your findings.

ACTIVITIES

These assignments are indicated by a *light bulb*. They give you practice in applying a certain format for thinking, one that's based on a cycle of observation, reflection, and judgment. The skills and approaches you use in both the exercises and the activities will be useful in practicing critical thinking beyond your involvement with this book.

1.
Mastering the Fundamentals

IN THIS CHAPTER

What is thinking?
Thinking is a purposeful mental activity.
You control it and not vice versa.

Critical thinking is crucial.
Critical thinking promotes success in school,
in business, and in living.

What is truth?
Truth is not something we create to fit our desires.
Rather, it is a reality to be discovered.

A helpful principle.
An idea cannot be both true and false at the
same time in the same way.

Recognize opinions.
Unlike facts, opinions are open to question
and analysis by critical thinking.

Test opinions.
Critical thinking means recognizing and
evaluating opinions.

Evaluate evidence.
Persuasive evidence demonstrates that one stated
opinion is more reasonable than another.

Dare to change your mind.
Critical thinkers form opinions carefully and are
willing to reconsider any opinion—even the most
cherished conviction.

A sample issue.
Consider astrology as a guide to everyday living
and see how critical thinking works.

**A comprehensive
thinking strategy.**
Observe, record your observations, and address
relevant questions.

What is

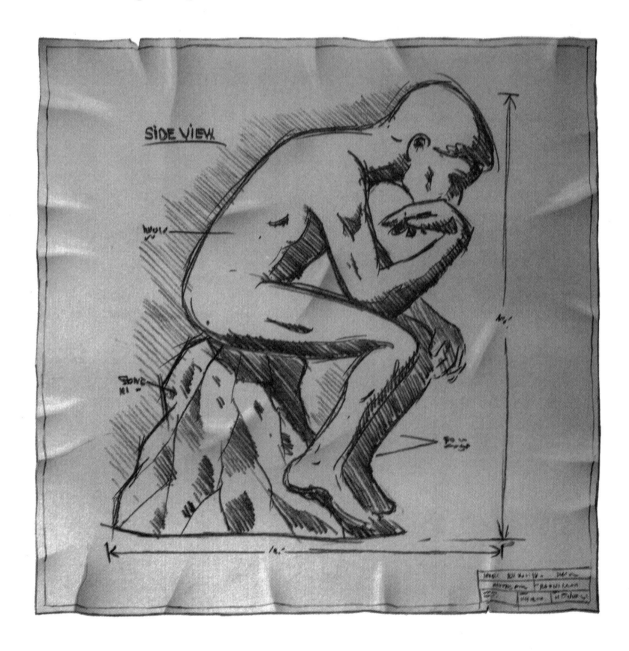

thinking?

Y OU ARE STARING into space, imagining you are headed for the airport. You picture yourself ready for a month's cruise in the Caribbean, your pockets stuffed with cash. Would this mental process be thinking?

Now imagine you're discussing politics with friends. "It's always the same with politicians," you say. "They're full of promises until they're elected. Then they develop chronic amnesia. I can't see why people get excited over elections." Would you be thinking in this case?

Thinking, as we will define it in this book, is a purposeful mental activity. You control it, not vice versa. For the most part, thinking is a conscious activity. Yet the unconscious mind can continue working on a problem after conscious activity stops—for example, while you sleep.

Given this definition, your ruminations about a Caribbean cruise are not thinking but daydreaming, merely following the drift of your fantasies. On the other hand, your discussion of politics may or may not involve thinking. We can't be sure. You might not be thinking at all but just repeating something you'd said or heard before.

Thinking is sometimes regarded as two harmonious processes. One process is the production of ideas (creative thinking), accomplished by *widening* your focus and looking at many possibilities. The key to this process is to resist the temptation to settle for a few familiar ideas. The other process is the evaluation of ideas (critical thinking), accomplished by *narrowing* your focus, sorting out the ideas you've generated, and identifying the almost reasonable ones.

Both processes are natural activities for human beings, but we rarely perform them well without training and diligent practice. This book focuses on evaluating ideas (critical thinking) but also includes some approaches for producing them.

Critical thinking is crucial

CHANCES ARE YOU'VE received little or no instruction in critical thinking. Your teachers are not to blame for this. In many cases they, and their teachers before them, were denied such training.

Much of our education was built on the idea that thinking can't be taught, or that some subjects teach it automatically. Modern research disproves both ideas. Thinking can be taught— not just to "gifted" students but to all students. No course automatically teaches thinking, though any course can teach it when teachers make thinking skills a direct objective. Then students get regular practice in producing and evaluating ideas. Around the world, schools are exploring ways to make critical thinking a priority.

Success in work depends on thinking skills. It isn't enough for graduates to possess a large body of information in their fields. People who want to succeed must be able to apply what they know to the challenges of their jobs. Employers are looking not for walking encyclopedias but for problem solvers and decision makers.

Mental health also depends in large part on skill in thinking. Some authorities believe neuroses stem from shallow, illogical thinking. According to psychologist Albert Ellis, "Man can live the most self-fulfilling, creative, and emotionally satisfying life by intelligently organizing and disciplining his thinking."

Unfortunately, shallow and illogical thinking is common. For example, the drug or alcohol abuser may say, "I'm not addicted—I can quit any time that I want." The skeletal anorexic may tell herself, "I'm too fat." Even highly educated people may reason, "My sexual partners are nice people, so I needn't fear catching a sexually transmitted disease."

Illogical thinking plays a big part in abusive behavior. A parent who makes a child cry by screaming at her may reason that hitting the child will make her stop crying. A Miami woman was recently charged with dousing her husband with rubbing alcohol and setting him on fire because he had been acting crazy and refusing to work. She reasoned that by setting him on fire she'd get him into the hospital for some help. A father kept his eighteen-year-old daughter chained in the basement because he was afraid she would become a prostitute.

Occasionally we read in the news about an attempted bank robbery that failed. Surely even slow-witted felons realize that banks have cameras and getaway cars can usually be identified. Also, every police agency, including the FBI, is involved in bank robbery investigations. Yet the robbers somehow manage to reach the conclusion that they will not be caught.

Even when poor thinking is not tragic, it can be embarrassing. Consider the man who loaned money to his friend, a car dealer. After trying unsuccessfully to collect the money, he reasoned: I'll take a car from his lot and hold it as collateral. Then he'll have to pay me to get his car back. Proud of his plan, he carried it out . . . and quickly found himself in jail on a charge of grand theft auto. Although the charge was dismissed, his humiliation lingered.

Much unpleasantness and disappointment can be avoided by testing ideas for reasonableness before accepting and acting on them. Such testing isn't just for special occasions. It is appropriate whenever someone makes a claim that is open to question. Many such assertions are made daily in every field of study and work.

Testing ideas is so fundamental to critical thinking that this book includes lots of practice in it. Throughout this book you'll encounter invitations to examine ideas for reasonableness. In many cases the ideas will be widely accepted in today's popular culture.

WHAT IS TRUTH?

The authors of popular books and magazine articles and celebrity guests on talk shows often make statements like the following: "There's no such thing as objective truth that's the same for all people regardless of their beliefs," "Truth is subjective and personal," and "Everyone creates his or her own truth." These people don't just mean that when we believe something to be true, we base our actions on that belief. No, they mean that believing something is so *actually makes it so!*

EXERCISE #1

Let's test this idea by considering situations where truth is considered important and asking whether this idea is reasonable.

SITUATION:

In the early seventeenth century, virtually everyone agreed that the sun revolved around the earth. Galileo shocked his contemporaries by arguing that the reverse was true. Is it reasonable to say that Galileo created a subjective truth, valid for him but not binding on other people? Explain.

_____

_____

_____

_____

_____

_____

SITUATION:

In the O. J. Simpson double murder trial, was the jury's assignment to create their own truth or discover the truth about what happened? Explain.

_____

_____

_____

_____

_____

_____

SITUATION:

Contemporary admirers of Hitler deny the existence of Nazi concentration camps and a Nazi plan to commit genocide against the Jews. Should that view be considered historically legitimate—true for those who wish to believe it? Why or why not?

_____

_____

_____

_____

_____

_____

SITUATION:

When Clarence Thomas was being considered for a seat on the U.S. Supreme Court, his former associate Anita Hill accused him of sexual harassment. Witnesses appeared before the Senate committee evaluating his candidacy. Would it have been appropriate for that committee to rule ,"Thomas has his truth, Hill has her truth, and both are equally valid"? Explain.

_____

_____

_____

_____

_____

_____

_____

SITUATION:

Throughout this century, a famous painting titled The Man with the Golden Helmet was believed to be the work of the Dutch master Rembrandt. Several years ago it was proved to have been painted by someone else. Some would say the truth about this painting changed. Explain your agreement or disagreement.

_____

_____

_____

_____

_____

_____

_____

_____

EXERCISE #2

Let's test this same view of truth further by considering how well it fits several everyday situations. Indicate "a" if the truth in this case is objective and discovered, and "b" if you think it is subjective and created. Be prepared to explain your choices.

_____A physician making a medical diagnosis.

_____A tax consultant preparing your income tax.

_____A laboratory researcher attempting to find a cure for cancer.

_____An archaeologist searching for a lost civilization.

_____A professor grading her students' homework.

_____A sports referee or umpire making a crucial call in a game.

_____An employer deciding who deserves a raise.

Exercise #3

Imagine you are explaining the concept of truth to a friend. What would you say? What examples (other than those mentioned in the previous two exercises) would you use?

_____
_____
_____
_____
_____
_____
_____
_____
_____
_____
_____
_____
_____
_____
_____
_____
_____
_____
_____
_____
_____
_____
_____
_____
_____
_____
_____
_____
_____

IF YOU DECIDED that in Exercises 1-3 the truth is objective and discovered, you'll be pleased to know that throughout the ages many scholars have shared your view. The traditional definition of truth is objective reality, the actual state of affairs about things.

According to this view, what people believe about something in no way alters reality. In other words, if a drunk dives into an empty swimming pool, thinking it is full won't soften his landing. If someone accidentally drinks poison believing it is Pepsi-Cola™, his belief won't diminish the harmful effects. College students are unlikely to make any headway with their instructors by arguing, "I thought my test answers were right, so you shouldn't take off credit." Admitting that truths of biology, psychology, and other subjects lie outside your control can make thinking more of an adventure. If the test of ideas is in the evidence rather than in your wishes, the challenge of forming ideas with care is greater and the reward for excellence is more meaningful.

A helpful principle

A GOOD WAY TO MAINTAIN a critical thinking perspective about ideas is to remember the principle of contradiction: **An idea cannot be both true and false at the same time in the same way.** Test this principle by examining a variety of statements and seeing whether they confirm it.

Statement: My roommate borrowed my sweater without permission.

Comment: If this statement were both true and false at the same time in the same way, it would mean that you simultaneously gave your permission and didn't give your permission. That is an impossibility. There may, of course, be an explanation for the disagreement—she may have misunderstood what you said to her. But that doesn't alter the fact that you either approved her taking the sweater or you didn't. It can't be both ways. Therefore this example confirms the principle of contradiction.

Statement: During World War II the Nazis killed six million Jews in concentration camps.

Comment: Either this holocaust happened or it didn't. Consider the thousands of photos, the written records, and the eyewitness testimony of both survivors and soldiers. Given this evidence, the neo-Nazi claim that the story is a Jewish lie is pathetic. But even more absurd is the idea that the holocaust happened and didn't happen. This example confirms the principle of contradiction.

Statement: There have been instances when little green creatures beamed uncooperative humans on board their space vehicles and conducted scientific experiments on them.

Comment: Even though we lacked the faintest notion of whether this ever happened, we can say with certainty that the answer must be either yes or no. (If it is no, that does not rule out the possibility that little *orange* creatures did so, or that the humans were *cooperative*.)

This statement also confirms the principle.

Statement: Capital punishment is a deterrent to crime.

Comment: Let's assume for the sake of discussion, that capital punishment was once a deterrent to crime but that it no longer is. In other words, that this statement was true at one time but is false today. Would this situation challenge the principle of contradiction? No. The principle of contradiction specifies that a statement cannot be both true and false *at the same time* in the same way.

Statement: Edgar is richer than Clem.

Comment: If Edgar has more money than Clem, but Clem surpasses him in moral character, then the statement would be both true and false, *but not in the same way*. It would be true in one sense but not in the other. That is not the same as saying Edgar has both more money and less money than Clem. Therefore this statement confirms the principle of contradiction.

The principle of contradiction keeps us aware that ideas sometimes directly contradict each other, and that we can't avoid contradiction by saying "Both sides are right." Even experts will occasionally disagree in their views. In such cases, we should consider the evidence and decide which view is right.

The principle of contradiction also reminds us that, even when contradiction isn't involved, ideas are seldom of equal quality. Solutions to problems range from practical to impractical, beliefs from well-founded to ill-founded, opinions from informed to uninformed, arguments from logical to illogical. Only by careful analysis can we separate the more worthy from the less and ultimately identify the best.

The principle of contradiction motivates us to excellence in critical thinking.

Recognize opinions

OPINIONS ARE BELIEFS or conclusions about reality. Unlike facts, they are open to question and analysis by critical thinking. Before evaluating opinions, first distinguish them from facts.

Sometimes it's easy to separate facts from opinions. "Babe Ruth was a famous baseball player" is clearly a fact. "Smoking should be banned in public places" is clearly an opinion. Yet many other statements are more difficult to classify.

Statement: The New York Knicks were the National Basketball Association champions in 1994.

Comment: This statement has the form of a fact. Yet it is not factual. The Houston Rockets defeated the Knicks to win the 1994 championship.

Statement: Camel's hair brushes are made of Siberian squirrel fur.

Comment: The statement appears ridiculous, yet it is factual.

Statement: Stalin's oppression of the Russian people was more brutal than Hitler's oppression of the German people.

Comment: This statement is an opinion, but it is so well supported by historical evidence that many would consider it a fact. (Stalin killed more of his own people than Hitler did. He also took away more freedoms for a longer period than did Hitler.)

Statement: Eyewitness testimony is generally unreliable.

Comment: This statement is an opinion. To those unfamiliar with the research on eyewitness testimony, it may seem untrue. Yet research confirms it.

Being able to recognize opinions will help you decide when an idea calls for support and what kind of support is appropriate. This knowledge can help you develop your own ideas and evaluate ideas from others.

Following are some basic guidelines:

1. If what you state is generally understood to be factual, no support is needed.

Example: Both John and Robert Kennedy were assassinated.

Example: The cost of a college education is significantly higher today than it was twenty years ago.

Comment: Both statements are common knowledge.

2. If what you state is not common knowledge or can't be easily verified, then briefly note the source of the information.

Example: The gray reef shark uses unusual body language to signal that it feels threatened.

Comment: This fact is not well known, at least among lay people, so cite the source. (It is Bill Curtsinger, "Close Encounters with the Gray Reef Shark," *National Geographic*, January, 1995, 45–67.)

3. If the statement is an opinion—a view others might disagree with—then answer any questions others might ask.

Example: More Americans are victimized by chronic laziness than by workaholism.

Comment: However reasonable this statement may seem, some people will undoubtedly disagree. Even those who agree may ask, Why does the author think this? What cases or examples support this view? Is statistical evidence available? Statements by authorities? What line of reasoning led the author to this conclusion? Unless these questions are satisfactorily answered, critical readers might not be persuaded.

4. If it is not clear whether a statement is a fact or an opinion, then treat the statement as an opinion.

Remember another important point about opinion. As used in critical thinking, opinion refers only to matters of judgment, not to matters of taste or personal preference. The ancient Roman saying *De gustibus non disputandum est* still holds true today. Loosely translated, this saying means, "There's no way to argue profitably or think critically about matters of taste."

Do you favor the now fashionable slender figure or the older ideal of plumpness? Do you find long or short hair more appealing? Do you wear formfitting athletic shorts or the long, baggy kind now standard in basketball? Do you regard the Lincoln Town Car as beautiful or ugly? Do you enjoy situation comedies more than soap operas? All these are matters of personal preference or taste. They can't be supported by facts but only by assertion—"That's my view because that's my view."

As long as you express matters of taste as such, you need not defend them, even if others find your tastes odd. If you express matters of taste as if they were matters of judgment, then you might be in the awkward position of defending what is difficult or impossible to defend. A solution is to say:

"I prefer slenderness to plumpness."
"I prefer long hair."
"I prefer formfitting athletic pants to long, baggy ones."
"I prefer the look of the Lincoln Town Car to that of any other car."
"I enjoy watching situation comedies more than soap operas."

Make statements like these instead of stating that one thing is superior to another.

EXERCISE #4
Indicate whether each of the following statements is

(a) clearly a fact.
(b) possibly a fact, but not clear without
    documentation.
(c) an opinion.
(d) a personal preference expressed as a
    personal preference.
(e) a personal preference incorrectly expressed
    as an opinion.

Remember, it is sometimes difficult to separate facts and opinions. There may be room for disagreement over some answers. Be prepared to explain your choices.

_____ 1. I like the shape of the new Pontiac Grand Am better than the shapes of most other new American cars.

_____ 2. Short, stocky men are more attractive than tall, thin men.

_____ 3. All religions share the same fundamental truths.

_____ 4. Darwin's theory of evolution continues to be controversial.

_____ 5. Religious history is filled with examples of inhumanity committed in the name of God.

_____ 6. Pornography is an insult to women.

_____ 7. In recent years, surgeons have performed successful procedures on fetuses still in the uterus.

_____ 8. Most women who have had abortions regret their decision.

_____ 9. Black people are the victims of crime more often than white people.

_____10. Prostitution should be legalized.

_____11. People who need organ transplants greatly outnumber donors.

_____12. The publicity given to suicides leads to most "copycat" suicide attempts.

_____13. Most students who drop out of school lack the intelligence to succeed.

_____14. During the O. J. Simpson trial, Judge Lance Ito favored the prosecution.

_____15. Comic books are as instructive about life as novels are.

EXERCISE #5

Now take the statements in Exercise #4 and do as follows:

- *For each that you classified b, state one or more reliable sources that could be cited to support the statement (assuming that the statement is factual).*

- *For each that you classified "C," write questions that might be raised about the statement.*

- *If you classified any statement "E," rewrite it as a personal preference rather than as an opinion.*

Test opinions

CRITICAL THINKING MEANS recognizing and evaluating opinions. Opinion has not always been held in the high regard it enjoys today. Almost 2,000 years ago, the Greek philosopher Epictetus wrote: "Here is the beginning of philosophy: a recognition of the conflicts between men, a search for their cause, *a condemnation of mere opinion* . . . and the discovery of a standard of judgment." Nineteenth-century British author Sir Robert Peel termed public opinion "a compound of folly, weakness, prejudice, wrong feeling, right feeling, obstinacy, and newspaper paragraphs."

American author John Erskine sarcastically termed opinion "that exercise of the human will which helps us to make a decision without information." George Santayana observed that "people are usually more firmly convinced that their opinions are precious than that they are true." And one humorist suggested that many opinions that are expressed ought to have gone by slow freight.

Why are these and many other observers so critical of opinion? Because opinions are so easy to form and shallow, foolish opinions are so difficult to change. Consider how long it took to change the opinions that the earth is flat, that slavery is acceptable, and that cigarette smoking is harmless.

Even experts, who know their subject in great depth, sometimes form erroneous opinions. It's not surprising that nonexperts err so easily.

Part of the problem is that it's difficult to acknowledge ignorance. People ask us what we think about something and we are reluctant to say, "I don't know." So we express a view and then bond with it, much the same as parents bond with a new baby. Rejecting the idea seems unthinkable. Over the years, we can accumulate hundreds or even thousands of opinions that we never test.

Armed with little more than a sketchy news report, an assertion by a celebrity, or a preconception, people state opinions on complex subjects: the cause of child abuse, the reason why dinosaurs became extinct, the benefits of supplemental vitamins, and many more.

Not long ago, a roving reporter took his tape recorder into the street and asked passersby, "How serious is racial tension in New York?" Among those who responded were a porter, two teachers, a truck driver, a film editor, a security guard, and a secretary. Even though these people may have known little about the matter, they still expressed an opinion.

There's a great difference between such casual, off-the-top-of-the-head opinions and informed opinions. For example, a physician's opinion about the best way to treat a disease is an informed opinion. So is an accountant's opinion about the legitimacy of a tax deduction, or the Supreme Court's decision on the constitutionality of a law. Critical thinkers in any field develop their opinions with care and test them for reasonableness.

Test some common opinions to see just how reasonable they are. To illustrate the testing process, consider a statement by a famous psychologist.

The Opinion: "One of the basic things which I was a long time in realizing, and which I am still learning, is that when an activity *feels* as though it is valuable or worth doing, it *is* worth doing." (Carl Rogers)

The Test: Think of a variety of activities that could conceivably feel valuable or worth doing and decide whether they *are* valuable or worth doing.

The Activities:

a. Sending a sympathy card to a friend whose parent just died.
b. Lying about your education and work experience on a résumé.
c. Lending money to your brother or sister.
d. Shoplifting.
e. Telling your parents how much you appreciate them.
f. Starting a nasty rumor about your ex-boyfriend or ex-girlfriend.
g. Seeing how fast your car will go.
h. Telling your boss what you think of him or her.

The Decision: Feelings sometimes guide us well (a, c, e) but sometimes do not (b, d, f, g, h). Therefore, Rogers's opinion is unsound.

This is not the only test we could conduct. Another would be to ask whether trusting feelings helps prejudiced people become fair–minded, wife beaters stop their abuse, or envious people overcome jealousy. We can also ask whether trusting feelings makes people more forgiving, marriages stronger, and neighborhoods safer. Since following feelings *leads* to such problems, it is unlikely to *solve* them.

Opinions can express important truths and serve as building blocks to knowledge. However, opinions can also confuse and mislead, obstructing genuine insights. Critical thinkers understand that having a right to an opinion does not mean that every opinion is right.

Carry out the test specified in each of the following Exercises.

EXERCISE #6

The Opinion: "With the right motivation anyone can achieve excellence in any field of endeavor."

The Test: Think of a variety of activities and a number of different people you know (or know of). Decide whether the opinion applies in their case.

The activities:

_____

_____

_____

_____

_____

_____

_____

_____

The decision:

_____

_____

_____

_____

_____

_____

_____

_____

EXERCISE #7

The Opinion: "You are the only thing that is real. Everything else is your imagination. . . . There are no victims in this life or any other. No mistakes. No wrong paths. No winners. No losers. Accept that and then take responsibility for making your life what you want it to be." (author Jack Hill)

The Test: (a) Think of one or more things, besides yourself, that are real rather than imaginary. (b) Think of one or more situations in which there are victims or mistakes or wrong paths or winners or losers. Then decide whether your findings confirm or refute the opinion.

The things/situations:

_____

_____

_____

_____

_____

_____

_____

The decision:

_____

_____

_____

_____

_____

_____

_____

_____

_____

EXERCISE #8

The Opinion: Movie star Demi Moore explained her decision to nurse her child until she was two years old: "That's a particular philosophy I have . . . allowing her to make her own decisions. I feel she is a better judge than I am."

The Test: Check what studies in child psychology reveal about a one- or two-year-old child's ability to decide. Visit the library and consult one or two child psychology books. Then decide whether Ms. Moore's opinion is reasonable.

The experts say:

_____
_____
_____
_____
_____
_____
_____
_____
_____

Your decision:

_____
_____
_____
_____
_____
_____
_____
_____

Evaluate evidence

It is possible to evaluate opinions even when they are stated alone, without supporting explanations. More commonly, though, people offer information to bolster their case. Such information, called evidence, comes in a variety of forms.

In informal writing and discussion, evidence may be nothing more than a simple statement of one or more reasons: "I believe this because. . . ." More often, evidence includes details about past events or incidents and references to observations or written accounts. Formal presentations frequently include experimental and statistical evidence, as well.

In evaluating evidence, the focus is not on the opinion itself but on the quality of the support that is offered. Persuasive evidence demonstrates that the stated opinion is more reasonable than others.

Example: That exam wasn't fair because it tested us on material that we were specifically told we weren't responsible for.
Comment: The evidence, if accurate, is persuasive. (Teachers have an obligation to keep their word.)

Example: I'm inclined to dismiss that story about Elizabeth Taylor as false. After it appeared in a supermarket tabloid, no other newspaper or broadcast agency picked it up.
Comment: The evidence, if accurate, is persuasive. Such tabloids have a reputation for misleading and exaggerated reporting. It is therefore reasonable to be cautious in accepting what they say, particularly when other news sources do not confirm the story.

Example: We acted properly in installing surveillance cameras in the employee lounge and restrooms because we have a right to identify troublemakers in the firm.
Comment: The evidence—the claim of a right to identify troublemakers—would be persuasive if no conflicting rights were involved. That is not the case. Employees also have the right of privacy. A more persuasive speaker would show that in this situation the employer's right outweighs the employees'.

Example: Taking money from my employer's petty cash fund isn't really stealing. My employer pays me less money than the person I replaced. He has also given me more responsibilities. And if I didn't take that money, I wouldn't be able to pay my bills.
Comment: Even if all three of the statements offered in support of the opinion are true, they are not persuasive. Stealing is defined as taking something belonging to someone else without that person's permission. The evidence offers an explanation of *why* the person stole (a weak explanation at that). But the act still constitutes stealing.

Even if the evidence presented is unpersuasive, the opinion could still be accurate. Other evidence that is not presented might be persuasive. Suppose a friend says to you, "That car salesman must be dishonest. He's just too smooth and accommodating." That evidence is unpersuasive. It's possible to be smooth, accommodating, and honest. Even so, the salesman may be dishonest. To decide whether he is, ask for more evidence than your friend presented. For example, find out whether the salesman accurately describes a car's features, available options, and safety ratings.

Familiarity can be a serious obstacle to critical thinking. When we agree with an opinion, we may easily approve any evidence offered in support of it. Conversely, when we disagree with an opinion, we may tend to reject even solid evidence. To judge evidence fairly, resist these tendencies. This task is difficult, calling for special care and attention.

EXERCISE #9

In each of the following cases, the first statement states an opinion, and the second sentence states supporting evidence. Decide whether the evidence shows that the stated opinion is more reasonable than any other. If the evidence is faulty and you have evidence that would support the opinion, state that evidence.

a. Your Honor, I believe I was justified in hitting my wife. She kept nagging me about getting a job.

_____

_____

_____

_____

b. I didn't sign that petition. The person who asked me to sign refused to support my proposal last year.

_____

_____

_____

_____

c. I oppose the health care proposal. It restricts people's freedom to choose their own physicians.

_____

_____

_____

_____

d. I recommend that we promote Martha rather than Bill. Our company doesn't have enough women in the upper levels of management.

_____

_____

_____

e. I oppose government funding for abortions. It requires taxpayers to finance a procedure that many of them believe is a moral outrage.

_____

_____

_____

_____

f. Students who are caught cheating should receive a failing grade in the course. Cheating is a serious violation of scholarly integrity.

_____

_____

_____

_____

g. Women should not take their husbands' names when they marry. Doing so is a sign of subjugation.

_____

_____

_____

h. Drugs should be legalized. Enforcing the nation's drug laws has proved an impossible task.

_____

_____

_____

_____

dare
to change your mind

CHANGING YOUR MIND means admitting that your prior view was mistaken. This admission is seldom pleasant, and many people go to great lengths to avoid it. But critical thinking demands that honesty be valued more than pleasant feelings, and that opinions be revised whenever the evidence suggests they are mistaken.

Some people have the idea that critical thinkers have no convictions. This idea is mistaken. It would be foolish for critical thinkers to take the time and trouble to find sound answers to important questions, and then refuse to embrace those answers with confidence.

If anything, critical thinkers prize convictions more highly than others do. They form opinions carefully and are willing to reconsider any opinion—even the most cherished conviction. This does not happen every time they encounter an opposing view, but whenever new evidence calls their view into question.

In contrast, uncritical thinkers form opinions casually. These thinkers treat every opinion as if it were a conviction and every conviction as if it were unquestionable. They applaud the wisdom of views that support their own. When uncritical thinkers encounter an opposing view, they become defensive and assert their opinions more forcefully. Hoping to avoid embarrassment, they actually increase it!

To avoid this mistake, keep the following facts in mind:

Your opinions and convictions do not own you; you own them. And any time you find an opinion to be lacking in quality, you have a right to discard it. When you change your mind and admit your mistake, you demonstrate courage and integrity.

If you form opinions carefully, you may often find that re-evaluation confirms them. That is to be expected.

But remember that everyone is wrong on occasion. So if your re-evaluation always confirms your original opinions, consider the possibility that you are unconsciously twisting the evidence in your own favor.

a sample issue

Consider an actual issue and see how a critical thinking approach works:

Jennifer begins to wonder whether her view of astrology is reasonable. Here is her view:

I think astrology is a good guide to everyday living. Newspapers, magazines, radio, and television treat it seriously. Many well-known, educated people use it to make decisions.

Seeking more evidence, Jennifer visits the library and discusses the project with the librarian. With his help, she finds a number of books and articles, some supporting astrology and others rejecting it. She also interviews a professor of psychology and a professor of comparative religion. After looking in the Yellow Pages, Jennifer calls a local astrologer.

After evaluating her reading and discussion, Jennifer changes her initial view. Her revised view and supporting evidence follow:

Many well-known, educated people believe in astrology. Even so, I think it's an ineffective guide to everyday living. One reason is that astrology is based on superstitions of a primitive time. For example: "Because Mars is red, it is associated with blood and aggression."

Another reason is astrology's argument that planets influence us at the moment of birth. Science has shown beyond question that the moment of conception is a more important time.

A third reason is that astrologers offer no answer to this question: If the planets Uranus, Neptune, and Pluto were discovered after 1780, weren't all horoscopes before that time necessarily wrong?

By having the courage to change her mind when the evidence called for it, Jennifer gained assurance that her opinion can withstand discussion and debate.

EXERCISE #10

State your present opinion on each of the following issues and the evidence for that opinion. Then re-evaluate your opinion. Consider alternative views. Gain additional evidence, and decide whether another view is more reasonable.

a. Should single-sex colleges and universities be allowed to receive federal funds?

_____
_____
_____
_____
_____

b. Should athletes be required to meet the same entrance standards as other students?

_____
_____
_____
_____
_____

c. Should term limits be set for all elective offices?

_____
_____
_____
_____
_____

d. Should condoms be made available to students in junior high schools?

_____
_____
_____
_____
_____

A comprehensive

ALL THE ASPECTS of critical thinking discussed in this chapter are important. Also important is an overall strategy for dealing with everyday situations. The strategy presented in this section can help you develop valuable insights and skills. It includes three steps:

1. Observe

2. Record your observations

3. Address relevant questions

Step 1: Observe

Good ideas spring more readily from a mind filled with knowledge than from an empty mind. The better you take note of the world around you, the better you can think. Picture your mind as a tree with branches reaching upward and outward. Branches grow only if the tree's roots extend deep and wide. Those branches are ideas; the roots are knowledge.

Knowledge comes through the senses, particularly sight and hearing. To observe means to detect the issues being discussed, the opinions expressed about those issues, the evidence offered in support of those opinions, and the various disputes that have arisen.

One arena for observation is printed material—newspapers, magazines, and books. Spend a little time each day keeping up with local, national, and world events. At the very least, consult the editorial pages of a good newspaper every day. Read the editorials, letters, and opinion columns. Don't read passively, waiting for understanding to jump out at you, but actively, looking for meaning.

In reading longer works, such as magazine articles and books, extend your concentration. Don't be discouraged if you encounter distractions. Everyone does. Concentrating is like driving a car down a curvy highway. We turn right, then left, making small corrections to keep the car on the road. Like a car, the human mind needs help to stay on course. You can direct your mind, making frequent adjustments as distractions arise. With practice, you'll become adept.

thinking strategy

A second arena for observation is nonprint media. These include movies, television, and radio. Many people tend to surrender their minds to these media more than to printed materials. That is a mistake. Strive to be as active a listener and viewer as you are a reader.

Yet another arena for observation is your everyday contacts with other people, at home, in school, and at work. Active listening here can bring you valuable knowledge and improve your personal relationships.

Several centuries ago, Francis Bacon argued that the purpose of reading is neither to agree nor to disagree with what is said but to weigh and consider it. That is good advice for all observation.

Step 2: Record your observations

Critical thinking entails reflecting on the meaning and significance of observations and the reasonableness of ideas. It would be nice if we could call a time-out whenever we wanted to reflect on something that happened or was said. Then life would come to a standstill until we were ready for it to resume.

Alas, we don't have that option. Time moves at its own pace. Hours may pass before we can spare time for reflection. By then we may have forgotten what happened or what about it we found interesting. That is why for most people the habit of reflection remains a good intention and not an accomplishment. A solution to this dilemma is to record interesting observations as they occur so that you can reflect on them.

The best way to do this is to keep a journal. This chapter will demonstrate how to do so and invite you to begin your journal. You'll find space at the end of each chapter for this kind of critical thinking practice and specific directions for doing it.

After you complete this book, you may wish to continue keeping a journal. Select a bound notebook no smaller than 6 x 9 inches. Use the left pages for recording observations and the right pages for reflections on those observations. Since reflections are often longer than observations, leave extra space between observations.

Here are kinds of observations to include and the kinds of reflection to aim for:

Observation: Interesting issues you would like to address when you have more time.

Reflection: Identify the various views people take on the issues and the evidence they offer in support. Find additional evidence, if possible, and decide which view of the issue is most reasonable.

Observation: Statements that appear to be unusually insightful. (The statements may have been made from authors, instructors, fellow students, or anyone else.)

Reflection: Think of appropriate ways to test the statements to determine whether they are in fact insightful. Carry out the tests. (Be prepared to modify or even reverse your first impression.)

Observation: Statements that seem to be shallow or mistaken. (The issue ought to be serious enough that the deficiencies of the statement are worth knowing more fully and perhaps responding to.)

Reflection: Think of appropriate ways to test the statements to determine whether they are in fact shallow or mistaken. Carry out the tests. (Be prepared to modify or even reverse your first impression.) If you wish, frame a response to any statement that proves to be shallow or mistaken.

Observation: Questions that arise from your reading, listening, or otherwise occur to you and seem worth pursuing.

Reflection: Decide how best to proceed in answering the questions. Answer them.

Observation: Ideas or situations that seem to have wider implications.

Reflection: Probe the implications.

Observation: Anything you experience or hear about that you wish to understand more fully. For example, an incident, a process or procedure.

Reflection: Decide how best to learn more about the matter. Apply yourself to that end.

Note that in all these situations your knowledge is incomplete or unsatisfactory. Statements or situations "appear" or "seem" to be one way or another, or you feel the need to understand "more fully." *Reflection begins when you admit ignorance and wish for knowledge.*

Step 3: Address relevant questions

The key to effective reflection is asking and answering relevant questions, as the following sample journal entries demonstrate. Note that the relevant questions are in italics.

Observation: Today I passed a house with a sign advertising psychic services— "Palm readings, Tarot cards, Your future foretold!" The house was in a rundown neighborhood. It occurred to me that all such places I've ever seen are in such neighborhoods. *Is that significant?*

Reflection: *What could a psychic accomplish if she used her powers to better herself?* She'd be able to make a fortune at the racetrack or in the stock market or the lottery and could afford to live in the most exclusive section of town. Psychics who live in poor neighborhoods could be unusually humble, refusing to use their powers for their own personal gain, or dishonest.

Observation: Newspaper advertisement: "Good news! Due to the unprecedented success of our giant end-of-year furniture sale, we have extended it for ten days." Somehow that doesn't sound logical.

Reflection: *Is my first impression accurate? Is there something amiss with this ad?* Let's see . . . *If the sale had been such a great success, wouldn't they have sold most or all of the furniture? If so, where are they getting the furniture for the extended period?* It doesn't make sense. Perhaps the truth is that the sale was such a flop that they were left with a store full of merchandise and have to extend the sale if they hope to get rid of it. *If this is the case, why didn't it sell? Are the prices too high? Is the quality too low?*

Observation: I read a magazine article about the violence that sometimes occurs at heavy metal rock concerts. The author said that it's unfair to blame the violence on the musicians or the music, and that human beings are naturally violent. This seems to make sense but I want to examine it more closely to be sure.

Reflection: If violence is due to human nature rather than heavy metal musicians and music, then it should occur just as often at other concerts. *What other kinds of musical events should I consider? How about square dances, polka or bluegrass festivals, Natalie Cole or Tony Bennett concerts, or the opera?* I can't remember ever seeing a newspaper headline that said, "Riot Mars Pavarotti Performance" or "Rowdy Polka Contestants Attack Bystanders." *Also, if violence is due to human nature, then shouldn't it be found in all societies and all groups within a society?* Yet incidents of violence are much more common in the United States than in Europe or Asia. And even within the U.S., violence is virtually unknown among the Amish. These thoughts force me to revise my first impression of the defense of heavy metal music and musicians. I don't know if they can be blamed for the violence at concerts, but they certainly can't be ruled out so conveniently.

Note that the three reflections exhibit imaginativeness. In the first case, the author moved from the observed context—psychic services being offered to others—to another context entirely—psychic services used for one's self. Imagining the new context led to the key thought, "Why don't they pick the winning horse, stock, or lottery number?"

In the second case, the author imagined how a store would look after a successful furniture sale—depleted of stock, perhaps even empty. In the third case, the author's imaginativeness was even more impressive, producing general categories of musical events, then specific examples, newspaper headlines, comparisons with Europe and Asia, as well as the example of the Amish.

In all three cases, imagination was stimulated by asking provocative questions. Use this approach to stimulate your imagination.

What about situations when you don't have all the information you need to make a judgment? On those occasions you will have to interrupt your reflection until you have obtained the information. One obvious source is the library. Librarians can direct you to books and other materials, as well as to knowledgeable people. Write down their suggestions so you'll have them for future use.

PRACTICING CRITICAL THINKING #1

Following are a sample observation and a suggestion for reflection. (Later Practicing Critical Thinking activities will give you less help.)

Observation

You read in an opinion essay: "Each culture decides for itself what is morally right and morally wrong. No one from outside a particular culture should criticize the moral standards of that culture." You've heard it before and it sounds reasonable but you wish to test the idea to be sure.

Reflection

(Suggestion for reflection: Think of situations in which one culture [or a person or group within a culture] criticized another culture. Decide whether in any of those situations the criticism was valid. Judge the above statement accordingly.)

_____
_____
_____
_____
_____
_____
_____
_____
_____
_____
_____

PRACTICING CRITICAL THINKING #2

Consider the following observation and suggestion for reflection. (Later Practicing Critical Thinking activities will give you progressively less assistance.)

Observation

You hear someone say, "I'm fascinated with the future because the future is where we're going to spend the rest of our lives."

Reflection

(Suggestion for reflection: Try to think of a specific occasion in which you spent time in the future. Discuss the implications of what you find or fail to find.)

_____
_____
_____
_____
_____
_____
_____
_____
_____
_____
_____
_____
_____
_____
_____

PRACTICING CRITICAL THINKING #3

In this case you are provided only with an observation. Decide what direction your reflection will take and proceed accordingly. (Consult the suggestions in "A comprehensive thinking strategy" if you wish.)

Observation

Line from a television commercial for a used car sales agency: "We'll cosign your loan even if you've had a bankruptcy. That's because we take the trouble to hand pick and inspect these cars before you even see them. . . .We guarantee financing because we only sell quality cars."

Reflection

_____
_____
_____
_____
_____
_____
_____
_____
_____
_____
_____
_____
_____
_____
_____
_____
_____
_____
_____
_____
_____
_____

PRACTICING CRITICAL THINKING #4

Reflect on the following observation as you did in previous Practicing Critical Thinking activities. (Consult the suggestions in "A comprehensive thinking strategy" if you wish.)

Observation

A guest on a self-help radio program makes the following statement: "In my counseling practice, I advise my clients to replace all their negative thoughts with positive ones. In other words, if they think 'I'm impatient,' they should say, 'No, I'm patient.' 'I'm clumsy' becomes 'I'm graceful,' and 'I'm a poor athlete' becomes 'I'm an excellent athlete.' I tell them that whatever they believe themselves to be, they will be."

Reflection

_____
_____
_____
_____
_____
_____
_____
_____
_____
_____
_____
_____
_____
_____
_____
_____
_____
_____

PRACTICING CRITICAL THINKING #5

Reflect on the following observation as you did in previous Practicing Critical Thinking activities.

Observation

When Budweiser Dry beer was introduced, a series of television commercials appeared on the theme "Why ask why? Try Bud Dry." The structure of the ad was to raise a few questions, such as "The Mona Lisa has no eyebrows. Why?" and "Chickens have no lips. Why?" and then to recite the slogan, "Why ask why? Try Bud Dry."

Reflection

_____
_____
_____
_____
_____
_____
_____
_____
_____
_____
_____
_____
_____
_____
_____
_____
_____
_____
_____
_____
_____
_____
_____
_____

PRACTICING CRITICAL THINKING #6

Reflect on the following observation as you did in previous Practicing Critical Thinking activities.

Observation

Talk shows often use air time to announce proposed future topics and solicit guests in this manner: "Do you secretly lust after your wife's mother? Call us. You may be selected for our show." This was an actual topic. Here are some others: "Are you sexually attracted to your children's babysitter?" "Is there someone you'd love to confront over a past offense?"

Reflection

_____
_____
_____
_____
_____
_____
_____
_____
_____
_____
_____
_____
_____
_____
_____
_____
_____
_____
_____
_____
_____
_____
_____
_____

PRACTICING CRITICAL THINKING #7

This activity will provide observations for use in later assignments. In each of the following categories, list as many observations as you can. Use additional paper if needed.

Interesting issues you would like to address when you have more time:

_____

_____

_____

_____

Statements that appear to be unusually insightful. (They may have been made by authors, instructors, fellow students, or anyone else.)

_____

_____

_____

_____

Statements that seem to be shallow or mistaken. Choose a statement serious enough that you want to know more about its flaws and perhaps respond to them.

_____

_____

_____

_____

_____

Questions that arise from your reading or listening or have otherwise occurred to you and seem worth pursuing.

_____

_____

_____

_____

Ideas or situations that seem to have wider implications.

_____

_____

_____

_____

_____

Anything you have experienced or heard about that you wish to understand more fully. Examples are an incident, a process, or a procedure.

_____

_____

_____

_____

_____

QUIZ

1 *This book focuses on evaluating ideas and also includes some approaches for producing them. True or false?*

2 *Why is critical thinking an important skill to develop?*

3 *Explain the error in this statement: "I create my own truth. What I believe to be true is true for me."*

4 *State the principle of contradiction. Then explain how this statement helps in critical thinking.*

5 *How can you help your readers in each of the following cases?*

   a) *You are making a statement that you know to be factual but not easily verified.*

   b) *You are making a statement that you are not certain is factual.*

   c) *You are making a statement others might disagree with.*

6 *Is it useful to argue about matters of taste? Explain your answer.*

7 *Respond to this statement: "I have a right to my opinion, so you have no business challenging it."*

8 *Define the term "evidence" and give some examples of it.*

9 *Do critical thinkers have convictions? Explain your answer.*

10 *State and briefly explain the three steps of the comprehensive thinking strategy presented in this chapter.*

2.
Becoming
an Individual

Understanding individuality.
By examining and changing your mental habits, you can become more of an individual.

Knowing your attitudes and values.
Even when we are unaware of attitudes and values, they exert a powerful influence on what we think, say, and do.

Knowing your mental habits.
One step to intellectual brilliance is understanding the usual ways you approach issues in school and everyday life.

Some characteristics of critical thinkers.
Critical thinkers look at themselves honestly, resist manipulation, ask questions, produce many ideas, base their judgments on evidence, acknowledge complexity, look for connections among ideas, and practice intellectual independence.

A COMMON MEANING of individuality is "uniqueness," a quality that sets a person apart from others. Even so, few people agree about when and how a person becomes an individual.

The popular notion is that everyone is an individual from conception and anything we think, say, or do expresses our individuality. Examine this idea to see if it makes sense. If everyone were unique, imitation would be rare. Indeed, it might not exist at all. We'd find little similarity in dress, speech patterns, and mannerisms, let alone in viewpoints.

Yet even a casual glance at people reveals a different picture. Count the number of young men's feet without socks and in hightop unlaced sneakers. Tally the number of designer labels on male or female behinds. Notice how many businessmen wear suits, shirts, and ties in the current style. See how many businesswomen have hemlines precisely where this year's fashion experts declare they should be.

Note speech patterns, observe mannerisms, listen to viewpoints on issues from abortion and capital punishment to taxation and welfarism. You're likely to see much more sameness than difference.

Such observations suggest that the popular notion of individuality is shallow. People are not born with individuality but with the potential to develop it. Likewise, what people say and do may not express individuality. Actions and words may simply express mindless conformity. Whether someone becomes an individual depends on the effort put into the task.

An early step in becoming an individual is to admit that we've been shaped by our culture. There's no shame in this. All of us experience this

Understanding

shaping force. When we were children, we learned from other people. This happened first with our parents and other relatives, later with teachers and peers. We accepted their explanations. We also adopted their attitudes—often without question.

During that same period, we may have seen thousands of hours of television. Small children have difficulty distinguishing between commercials and program content. So as children we probably viewed the ravings of a used car salesman with the same trust we placed in the weather report. More important, uncritical viewing easily becomes a habit. Perhaps we still have our intellectual guard down whenever we watch television.

Many of the attitudes, values, and ideas we regard as an essential part of ourselves were probably formed before we were mature enough to understand them. Perhaps many seemed so familiar that we never questioned them. These are not pleasant conclusions about ourselves, but they are inescapable.

Once we've admitted that some of our attitudes, values, and ideas are borrowed uncritically from others, we can appreciate the importance of discovering where we got them. What's more, we can decide whether we want to keep them.

This intention is key to becoming and remaining an individual. Your environment will continue to shape you as long as you live, so this process of evaluation will never end.

While doing the Exercises in this chapter, you may be tempted to pretend that you're not influenced by others. If you give in to this temptation, you fool yourself and miss the opportunity to become the person you'd like to be.

individuality

Knowing your attitudes and values

ATTITUDES ARE NOT THOUGHTS or actions but rather *tendencies* to think or act in certain ways. We are seldom aware of our attitudes in the way we are aware of our ideas. Attitudes reside more in the shadows than in the brighter regions of the mind. Yet they can exert a powerful influence on what we think and say and do.

Consider the attitude "I am more important than other people." People who have this attitude seldom express it directly, yet what they say and do reveals it. They may demand kindness, sensitivity, and loyalty from others but never practice these virtues; break dates when they wish but resent their friends' doing so; expect apologies but never offer them.

Many of our attitudes come from our environment rather than our genes. Americans raised abroad—say in Nigeria, France, China, or Argentina—are likely to have different attitudes than Americans raised in the United States. The religious, social, and political realities of those countries will influence their perspective, sometimes subtly, sometimes more obviously.

Some people suggest that the main reason why many Asian boys and girls excel in school is the positive attitudes they have toward parents, teachers, and learning. Likewise, these people believe that the main reason why many other youngsters do poorly is that they lack these attitudes.

In late twentieth-century America, popular culture is influencing attitudes more than ever. As we noted in Chapter One, modern entertainment often presents the idea that truth is created rather than discovered, and that everyone has his or her own truth. Constant repetition of this idea persuades many people that whatever they think must be right, merely because they think it. This can pose a great obstacle to critical thinking.

Values are principles, standards, or qualities considered worthwhile or desirable. We all have many values, even if we never analyze them. Specific values and their order of importance differ from person to person. For some people, integrity is the highest value. Faced with a choice between following their conscience and being highly regarded by their peers, they would choose honesty. For other people, no value is higher than what others think of them.

Popular culture exerts a subtle but powerful influence on our values. A steady diet of scandalous news stories—about Joey Buttafuoco, Michael Jackson, John Wayne Bobbitt, O. J. Simpson, and others—can affect the mind much the same way caffeine affects the body. For many people, sensationalism is not just another value but a positive craving.

During the 1994 Winter Olympics, the news media finally decided that the United Nations' ultimatum to Serbia was slightly more important than whether Tonya Harding and Nancy Kerrigan shared the same practice rink in Lillehammer, Norway. After that decision, news of that scandal ceased abruptly for a few days. As a result, people who were absorbed in the Harding-Kerrigan drama suddenly experienced the gnawing feeling that their lives had been disrupted.

Attitudes and values often program opinions. A person who feels hostile toward minorities is more likely than others to believe the worst when a black or Hispanic person receives a promotion. People who strongly value self-reliance might oppose assistance programs for poor people, especially if they feel that poverty is blameworthy. A person who values respect for elders will take the problem of rudeness more seriously than others do.

Like attitudes, values affect the quality of our thinking. If we value consistency more highly than truth, we will hesitate to change our minds, even when sound reasoning calls on us to do so. If we assign our feelings a higher priority than evidence, the quality of our reasoning is likely to suffer.

One crucial step to becoming a critical thinker is evaluating your attitudes and values. The purpose of the following Exercises is to help you with that evaluation. These Exercises work best if you respond directly and honestly. *Don't screen out any ideas or change them to fit what you think others might want you to say.* If you turn in these Exercises, be sure to save them when your instructor returns them to you. Later Exercises will build on what you write here.

> **There are times when the greatest change needed is a change of my viewpoint.**
>
> **—C. M. Ward**

EXERCISE #11

Record your first thoughts on each of the following subjects in the space provided. Include statements that support your views.

Keeping promises

_____

_____

_____

Being on time

_____

_____

_____

Schoolwork vs. socializing

_____

_____

_____

Unfamiliar situations

_____

_____

_____

Good manners

_____

_____

_____

Personal appearance

_____

_____

_____

Rooting for the underdog in sports, politics, etc.

_____

_____

_____

Success in life

_____

_____

_____

Authority

_____

_____

_____

Discipline

_____

_____

_____

Celebrities

_____

_____

_____

Intellectuals

_____

_____

_____

Life after death

_____

_____

_____

Right and wrong

_____
_____
_____

Patriotism

_____
_____
_____

The Golden Rule: "Do unto others as you would have them do unto you"

_____
_____
_____

Friendship

_____
_____
_____

Drugs and alcohol

_____
_____
_____

Excellence

_____
_____
_____

Hard work

_____
_____
_____

Religion

_____
_____
_____

Love

_____
_____
_____

Marriage

_____
_____

Teachers

_____
_____

Parents

_____
_____
_____

Beauty

_____
_____
_____

Knowing your mental habits

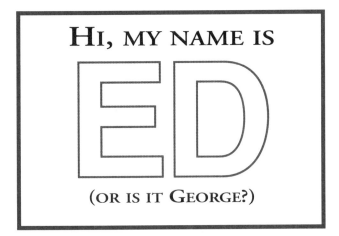

HI, MY NAME IS ED
(OR IS IT GEORGE?)

YOU'RE AT A PARTY and notice several people standing near you. One of them says, "Betty, meet George." You're shocked. That guy's name isn't George, you think. It's Ed. Later, you seek the person who made the introduction and ask him if he made a mistake. He assures you he didn't.

As the evening wears on, you hear other people saying "George" this and "George" that. You reflect on the dozens, hundreds of times you've called him Ed. Apparently he was too polite to correct you. Your face flushes with embarrassment at the thought. "How could I have been so dumb?" you say over and over to yourself.

It's a matter of being not dumb, just unobservant. Many people get so lost in their own internal reverie that they don't see or hear much else. Some people who love Seinfeld and wouldn't miss an episode manage to mispronounce his name as "Steinfeld." All the times they heard his name pronounced on the show and saw it spelled out in the credits made no impression on them.

Intellectual excellence calls for certain mental habits—being alert to what is going on around us, actively seeking out insights, controlling the tendency to leap to conclusions, and thinking before speaking and acting. One step in improving your mental habits is assessing them. Following are some Exercises to help you understand the usual ways you approach issues in school and everyday life.

EXERCISE #12

Read each of the following statements one at a time. Notice what happens as you read them and immediately afterward. Perhaps you'll hear the words or see them in your mind. It might seem as if they're on a screen, with one word more clearly in focus than the others. Perhaps you'll produce a vivid mental picture. Or perhaps you'll move quickly to some association or experience. A happy, say, or angry feeling might rise up in you. These responses are clues to your mental habits.

Here's a useful strategy for this assignment. Write your immediate response to the statement. Expand that response if you can. Then look back at what you've written and describe the process of thinking or feeling as it unfolded.

Consider the following example.

A sample statement:
Trend is not destiny.
—Lewis Mumford

An immediate response:
Trend *means the way a person or many people are heading or behaving. Destiny is what a person and his or her life are meant to be. So what does this statement mean? That my thoughts and actions aren't the only possible ones, even if they feel as if they are. I can choose against the force of habit or peer pressure. For example, I don't have to wear the "in" clothes or agree with the most popular ideas. I can assert my individuality. Mumford's idea makes sense to me.*

An analysis of the immediate response:
In this case my first reaction was to go over in my mind what the key words of the sentence mean. Then I restated the sentence to recapture its full meaning. Next came to mind an example of how the idea applies in my life. Finally, I decided I agreed with it.

Success is a journey, not a destination. —Ben Sweetland

_____
_____
_____
_____
_____

Many people's tombstones should read "Died at 30. Buried at 60." —Nicholas Murray Butler

_____
_____
_____
_____

Women should remain at home, sit still, keep house, and bear and bring up children. —Martin Luther

_____
_____
_____
_____

Victory has a hundred fathers, but defeat is an orphan. —Count G. Ciano

_____
_____
_____
_____

I do not believe in the collective wisdom of individual ignorance. —Thomas Carlyle

_____
_____
_____
_____
_____

EXERCISE #13

Describe your reactions to the following situations, as you did in Exercise #12. Include your typical feelings, thoughts, words, and actions.

a. *You express a point of view in a conversation and a friend disagrees with you.*

b. *You're in a large class and the teacher calls on you.*

c. *You're doing a homework assignment and are unsure of how to proceed.*

d. *You're listening to someone you don't like. He's talking to a group of your friends, and they seem interested in what he's saying.*

e. *You begin reading a book or an article on a subject you feel strongly about. Then you realize the author's view strongly opposes yours.*

EXERCISE #14

List (1) the books, magazines, and newspapers you most enjoy reading, (2) the courses of study that most interest you and why, (3) the courses of study you find least interesting and why.

EXERCISE #15

While doing a reading assignment for one of your courses, answer these questions:

• What is your typical way of approaching such an assignment? Do you plunge right in or skim it first? If you skim, what specifically do you look for?

_____

_____

_____

_____

• How long can you maintain your attention before you're distracted?

_____

_____

_____

• What kinds of distractions bother you more—external distractions or those in your own mind?

_____

_____

_____

_____

EXERCISE #16

Have you ever made any statements like the following? If so, describe when and where you made the statement. Identify the mental habit associated with your reaction.

"This course is unimportant because it's not required for my major."

_____

_____

_____

"This instructor is assigning far too much work."

_____

_____

"It's only fair for the instructor to put something on the test if she says we're responsible for knowing it."

_____

_____

"If the class gets too tough, I'll drop it."

_____

_____

_____

"The reason I'm doing poorly is that the teacher doesn't like me."

_____

_____

_____

"Students who take part in class discussions are just trying to make an impression on the teacher."

_____

_____

_____

Exercise #17

How effectively do you respond to challenges? Are your reactions more emotional than rational, or the reverse? Describe situations that support your judgment.

Exercise #18

Look back over the Exercises 11–16 that you completed when you read "Knowing your attitudes and values" and "Knowing your mental habits." Examine your responses and find the attitude, value, or idea each reveals. Decide how you acquired that attitude, value, or idea. Write your conclusions on photocopies of the original pages or below.

Some characteristics of critical thinkers

CRITICAL THINKERS differ from other people in a number of ways. The first sections of this chapter helped you develop one of them: self-knowledge. Philosophy is said to have begun in Socrates' directive "Know thyself." The wisdom of that directive has remained strong over the 2,500 years since he first expressed it. Knowing your own mind is one step in using it effectively.

Critical thinkers are uncommon in other ways, too. By understanding the qualities of such individuals, you can learn to think more effectively. Following are some important qualities.

Critical thinkers are honest with themselves

Through uncritical thinking, people deceive themselves. They pretend that the truth is what they wish it to be. They persuade themselves that they can drive 30 miles per hour over the speed limit without endangering themselves or others. They think drinking a six-pack of beer each day is no signal of a drinking problem, or that missing class has no effect on grades. They believe that hotel managers expect guests to steal towels, and that copying computer programs is morally acceptable. When someone disagrees, they dismiss the challenge immediately.

Critical thinkers avoid such maneuvers. They acknowledge even unpleasant ideas. If they do something foolish or immoral, they refuse to compound the mistake by pretending it was sensible or moral. When they hear a valid argument, they accept it—even if that means rejecting a cherished personal view.

Critical thinkers' honesty with themselves comes from admitting their limits. They know that to be human is to be fallible. They know that "knowledge" in most cases is an assortment of facts, assumptions, interpretations, and conclusions. So they are careful to limit their claims to certainty.

This perspective is not popular today. We are told we should be confident, trust our judgment implicitly, and assert our views without reservation. Intellectual humility is often considered a handicap. This idea can lead many people to express an opinion on matters they know little or nothing about.

During the O. J. Simpson trial, for example, prosecuting attorney Marcia Clark was in the midst of a divorce. The only details on public record were these: her husband was asking for custody of their two children, Ms. Clark's work schedule during the trial was a grueling sixteen hours a day, six or seven days a week, and her income was twice that of her husband.

Producers of the television show *Hard Copy* polled its audience on the question "Should Marcia Clark's children stay with her during the Simpson trial?" Despite the lack of public information, thousands of people expressed their opinions, two-thirds of them answering yes. One woman went so far as to declare, "I believe she's spending quality time with her children when she sees them" (*Hard Copy*, NBC-TV, March 8, 1995).

Critical thinkers resist the temptation to feign knowledge. They'd be more apt to say, "Before I answer that question, I want to know a lot more about Ms. Clark, her husband, the children, and how the children are cared for." Critical thinkers realize that admitting ignorance is a powerful step toward gaining knowledge.

Critical thinkers resist manipulation

The desire to be admired and accepted   by others can make us easier to manipulate. Advertisers know it, and they design ads to play on this desire. They promise that lipstick or aftershave lotion will make us irresistible. They also tell us that cars, clothes, or toilet bowl cleaners will make us the envy of the neighborhood.

Three of the most common themes used in media to manipulate the public are: (1) Self-indulgence. The appeal here is "Don't deny yourself this [product or service]. Go ahead and treat yourself. You deserve it."

(2) Impulsiveness. This appeal is "Don't delay. Don't pause to think and evaluate. Just act." And, (3) Instant gratification. The appeal here is "Why wait? You can enjoy it now and it will make you feel s-o-o-o-o good."

Advertisers aren't the only ones who use these and other forms of manipulation. People who want to sell us their ideas or proposals—such as politicians—often manipulate our thinking rather than use honest persuasion.

We can defend against manipulation by admitting that we are vulnerable to it and staying alert to detect it.

Critical thinkers overcome confusion

Like everyone else, critical thinkers are sometimes confused. What sets critical thinkers apart is that they don't stay confused. When they can look up something in a reference book or check with an authority, they take the initiative. They find an answer.

Many times all that is needed is more careful thinking. When critical thinkers meet a sentence whose meaning eludes them, they consider a number of possible meanings. Then they choose the most likely one.

Suppose a critical thinker has difficulty understanding the meaning of this proverb: "The girl who can't dance says the band can't play." She wonders, Is the reference here to dancing or t o other situations as well? Just how broad is its meaning? Then she considers how the proverb applies to other situations: a small boy having trouble catching the ball and blaming the thrower; a student having trouble with a course and blaming the teacher. Finally, the critical thinker concludes that the proverb covers a wide variety of situations and might be paraphrased, "People tend to blame others for their own shortcomings."

Critical thinkers ask questions

Critical thinkers realize that it's easy to make shallow, inaccurate statements. So when they're dealing with ideas, they ask penetrating questions to test the ideas.

Here is a viewpoint, followed by questions a critical thinker might ask. The question numbers correspond to the sentence numbers.

Viewpoint:
(1) I'm disappointed with the instructors at this university. They seem content to offer uninteresting courses. (2) For example, they stand at the lectern and lecture all period without enthusiasm for their material. (3) On the rare occasions when they open discussion to the class, they call on the same few students. (4) The rest of us have to sit squirming, waiting for the boring ordeal to be over. (5) I wish the faculty at this institution cared enough to make their classes interesting.

Questions:
1. How likely is it that the writer knows all or most of the instructors at this university?
2. How likely is it that all or most of the instructors teach strictly by lecture and without enthusiasm?
3. Why are the same few students always called on (assuming this claim is accurate)? Do these students raise their hands and show an interest in the questions? Do other students, including this writer, ever volunteer a comment or question?
4. Are all but a few students at this university really so bored? Or has the writer projected his reaction on them? Is it possible that the students who squirm have overly negative attitudes?
5. Whose responsibility is it to make a class interesting? The instructor's alone? Do the students bear any responsibility?

Critical thinkers take the time to produce many ideas

Many people are idea-poor. For each challenge that confronts them, they have a single answer, often the first one that pops into their minds or one they see in print or hear on television. With that approach, the odds of their producing powerful ideas are slender.

When the price of a postage stamp was raised from 29 to 32 cents, people with a supply of the cheaper stamps had to combine them with three-cent stamps. The lines at post offices in some areas were unusually long, and the demand for three-cent stamps quickly exceeded the supply. One reason was that some people bought many more stamps than they needed. For example, people who needed ten three-cent stamps bought 50 or 100. Perhaps they believed the stamps would increase in value.

It got even sillier. One man entering a post office saw the sign "Sorry, we're temporarily out of three-cent stamps." He grumbled in displeasure and said as he walked away, "I've driven to four post offices and they're all out of stamps. Now I've got to try a fifth." Apparently he never considered other options. He could have walked up to the window, bought some four-cent stamps—plenty were available—and mailed his letters.

One key to producing lots of ideas is to defer judgment and produce lots of ideas before embracing any one. Extend your effort to identify possibilities. A helpful technique is **springboarding**. Here's how it works: Think of an idea and add to it right away. Resist the urge to dwell on details. Don't worry about writing complete sentences; a word or short phrase will do. Use one idea to propel you to others. To keep the process going, end each item in your list with the word *and*.

Say that the subject you are addressing is students' attitudes in class. Your list of ideas might be as follows. Note how asking questions cues you to continue springboarding. The cue questions below are italicized.

Attitudes in Class

What Attitudes?
    disinterest in class and
    hostility to teacher and . . .

Are There More?
    disapproval of students who speak and
    uncooperativeness in class discussion and
    disrespect for other students and . . .

How Are Attitudes Revealed?
    smirking and
    whispering while others are talking and
    arriving late for class and
    making rude remarks and
    doing unrelated things like cleaning nails, and . . .

Why Do Students Do These Things?
    to maintain a "tough" image and
    to hide fear of failing and
    to make teachers uncomfortable and . . .

What Are Some Favorable Attitudes?
    cooperativeness and
    willingness to listen to others' viewpoints and
    patience when the discussion gets complex and . . .

How Are These Attitudes Revealed?
    looking at the person speaking and
    waiting for her to finish before you speak and
    refraining from side discussions and
    emphasizing the positive and . . .

The list could go on. You could think about how some students develop positive attitudes and others develop negative ones. Or you might explore how teachers can effectively deal with students who have negative attitudes.

Here is an additional tip: be open to ideas at all times. You may find that insights occur to you when you don't expect them—while you shower, walk from class to class, or even fall asleep at night. Perhaps you said to yourself on some of these occasions, "I've got to remember this idea later," and found later that you had forgotten it.

To capture ideas, keep a pen and paper handy. That way you can record ideas when they occur. Once you start doing so, chances are you'll be rewarded with many more ideas.

Critical thinkers base their judgments on evidence

Many people pay little attention to the need for evidence. In fact, they often form their views first and seek support for them later. Critical thinkers weigh the evidence before making a judgment. And if they have a bias toward a particular view, they make a special effort to be fair-minded.

Critical thinkers know what kind of evidence and how much of it they need. They raise relevant questions about the issue. (See "Critical thinkers ask questions.") They also seek answers to those questions. When they've done this and identified any conflicts in the evidence, they're ready to form a view.

Critical thinkers acknowledge complexity

Critical thinkers know that in controversial issues the truth is often complex. They make judgments to reflect that complexity. For example, ask several people, "Do you think today's politicians are honest?" You may hear one of these replies:

They're crooks, obviously, hypocrites, the lot of them.
All politicians disgust me.

Critical thinkers recognize that neither of these answers does justice to the question. They're more likely to say: *"Some politicians are dishonest. Still, there are likely many honest, dedicated politicians as well. I choose to consider each person separately."*

Critical thinkers are not mechanical in their thinking. Being human, they experience the same emotional reactions and temptations to snap judgment and overstatement as anyone else. Yet critical thinkers make a conscious effort to control those reactions and avoid those temptations. Before they express a view, they take the trouble to be sure it is responsibly formed.

Critical thinkers look for connections between subjects

Schools and colleges have English departments, history departments, chemistry departments, and so on. Over the centuries, educators found it convenient to organize knowledge that way. Unfortunately, some students assume that all their subjects fall into neat compartments. These students don't try to connect what they learn in one subject with what they learn in another. That notion prevents them from becoming critical thinkers.

Critical thinkers realize that concepts and strategies learned in one subject often apply to other subjects. What's more, they know that most serious problems touch many fields. AIDS, for example, creates not only medical challenges but psychological, legal, and moral challenges as well.

Critical thinkers are intellectually independent

To many people, intellectual independence means, "I'll do everything my own way. I'll ignore what others think and do." This perspective hinders learning and is self-defeating. Life is too short for learning all we need to know solely through our own experience. Ideas from others can make us dependent only if we accept them without thinking.

Realizing this, critical thinkers are eager to learn from others' experience. They seek out and consider a wide spectrum of ideas on important issues. Then they make their own judgments. Critical thinkers also reassess views when new evidence comes to light. Each of these habits promotes intellectual independence.

EXERCISE #19

Think of a time when you pretended that you knew something that in fact you did not know. Would you have gained by being more honest about your ignorance? If so, in what way?

_____
_____
_____
_____
_____
_____
_____
_____
_____
_____
_____
_____
_____
_____
_____
_____
_____
_____
_____
_____
_____
_____
_____
_____
_____
_____

EXERCISE #20

Give one or more examples of advertisements that use the following themes:

Self-indulgence

_____
_____
_____
_____
_____
_____
_____
_____

Impulsiveness

_____
_____
_____
_____
_____
_____
_____

Instant gratification

_____
_____
_____
_____
_____
_____
_____

EXERCISE #21

Think of current social problems in this country that could be linked to the themes mentioned in Exercise #20. List those problems and explain the linkage.

EXERCISE #22

Think of an occasion when you were manipulated. Describe how it happened. Explain specific steps you can take to avoid being manipulated in the future.

Exercise #23

Explain in your own words what each of the following sayings means. If you aren't sure of the meaning, overcome your confusion by identifying possible meanings and deciding which is most plausible.

A cathedral, a wave of a storm, a dancer's leap, never turn out to be as high as we had hoped. —Marcel Proust

_____

_____

_____

_____

_____

_____

_____

Happiness is not a state to arrive at, but a manner of traveling. —Margaret Lee Runbeck

_____

_____

_____

_____

_____

_____

_____

_____

Men are not punished for their sins, but by them. —Elbert G. Hubbard

_____

_____

_____

_____

_____

_____

_____

_____

Exercise #24

Read each of the following viewpoints carefully. Then write pertinent questions in the space provided.

Viewpoint 1: (1) Some people believe that professional wrestling should be seen as an entertainment rather than a sport. I disagree. (2) Professional wrestling demands athletic skill. (3) It involves competition so intense that it often results in physical injury. (4) I admit it is entertaining, but so are football, boxing, and tennis. (5) If the critics dared to enter the ring with a professional wrestler, they'd quickly learn that wrestling is not mere entertainment.

_____

_____

_____

_____

_____

_____

_____

_____

Viewpoint 2: (1) Far from being harmful, reading pornographic literature or watching pornographic films could be healthy. (2) Such material helps young people learn about sex. (3) It provides enjoyment to millions of men and an increasing number of women. (4) And these materials break down the puritanism that has caused our rising divorce rate.

_____

_____

_____

_____

_____

_____

_____

_____

EXERCISE #25

Answer each of the following questions with your tentative viewpoint and supporting evidence. On a separate sheet of paper make each response at least several sentences long. Then ask questions about these viewpoints as you did in Exercise #24 and list those questions in the space provided below.

a) *Can animals think?*

Your questions:

_____
_____
_____
_____
_____
_____
_____
_____
_____

b) *Should gambling be legalized?*

Your questions:

_____
_____
_____
_____
_____
_____
_____
_____
_____

c) *Should teachers be allowed to spank elementary school children who misbehave in school?*

Your questions:

_____
_____
_____
_____
_____
_____
_____
_____
_____
_____
_____

d) *Do smokers discount the evidence that smoking can kill them?*

Your questions:

_____
_____
_____
_____
_____
_____
_____
_____
_____
_____
_____

EXERCISE #26

List one or more situations in which an idea you embraced proved later to be shallow or unworkable.

_____
_____
_____
_____
_____
_____
_____
_____
_____
_____
_____
_____
_____
_____
_____
_____
_____

EXERCISE #27

Consider each of the following statements. Decide whether each is completely true, partly true, or completely false. Don't just accept your first reactions; decide if those reactions are reasonable. If you find any statement partly true, explain in what way it's true and in what way it is not.

People ask you for criticism but they only want praise.
—W. Somerset Maugham

_____
_____
_____
_____
_____

Wise men learn more from fools than fools from wise men.
—M. P. Cato

_____
_____
_____
_____
_____
_____

The offender never forgives. —Russian proverb

_____
_____
_____
_____
_____
_____

No matter which side of an argument you're on, you always find some people on your side that you wish were on the other side. —Jascha Heifetz

_____
_____
_____
_____

EXERCISE #28

On a separate sheet of paper, write about one of the following issues. Decide what you think about that issue and list the evidence for your view. Next seek other views and additional evidence. Then decide which view is most reasonable. In doing this Exercise, make an effort to demonstrate the characteristics of the critical thinker explained in this chapter. Then write a paper of at least several paragraphs persuading the reader to accept your view. (You may wish to consult the article "Expressing your ideas persuasively" in Chapter Five.)

a) Is it wrong to criticize another person's view of a controversial issue?

b) Do you favor subjecting animals to painful experiments in order to find cures for diseases?

c) Do you believe that atheists can be as moral as religious believers?

d) Why is the rate of violent crime so high in American society, compared to the rate in other industrialized societies?

e) Do you favor allowing women to become priests, ministers, or rabbis?

f) Would you favor mandatory prison terms for people convicted of drunken driving?

g) Do you think it is a good idea to abolish compulsory attendance laws in the nation's high schools?

PRACTICING CRITICAL THINKING #8

Look back at the list of observations you prepared in response to Practicing Critical Thinking #7 in Chapter One. Select one of those observations, restate it below, and then add your reflections, as explained in Chapter One. Observations, remember, are interesting issues, statements that appear insightful (or mistaken), probing questions, ideas that may have wider implications, or anything else that you wish to understand more fully, such as incidents, processes, or procedures. Reflections are your thoughtful analyses of the observations.

Observation

_____

_____

_____

_____

_____

Reflection

_____

_____

_____

_____

_____

Practicing Critical Thinking #9

List below any observations you made since you completed your response to Practicing Critical Thinking #7 in Chapter One. (Note: this activity will be repeated at the end of other chapters. If you make any observations between chapters, record them in the following chapter.)

Interesting issues you would like to address when you have more time.

_____

_____

_____

_____

_____

Statements that appear to be unusually insightful. (They may have been made by authors, instructors, fellow students, or anyone else.)

_____

_____

_____

_____

_____

_____

Statements that seem to be shallow or mistaken. Choose a statement serious enough that you want to know more about its flaws and perhaps respond to them.

_____

_____

_____

_____

Questions that have arisen from your reading or listening or have otherwise occurred to you and seem worth pursuing.

_____

_____

_____

_____

_____

Ideas or situations that seem to have wider implications.

_____

_____

_____

_____

Anything you have experienced or heard about—for example, an incident, a process, or a procedure—that you wish to understand more fully.

_____

_____

_____

_____

Name_____Date_____/_____/_____

1 *Write your viewpoint on this statement: "Everyone is born an individual and everything a person says or does is an expression of his or her uniqueness." Offer some evidence to support your viewpoint.*

2 *What is the first step in becoming an individual as explained in this chapter?*

3 *According to this chapter, what is the key to becoming and remaining an individual?*

4 *What are attitudes and how do we get them?*

QUIZ

C O N T I N U E D

5 *What are values?*

6 *Do people's values affect the quality of their thinking? Explain your answer.*

7 *According to this chapter, much of what is regarded as intellectual excellence is a matter of having good mental habits. True or false? Explain your answer.*

8 *This chapter discussed several characteristics of critical thinkers. One of them is self-knowledge. List the others.*

3.
Evaluating Longer Arguments

IN THIS CHAPTER

What is an argument?
Arguments express lines of reasoning, and you can use the four steps explained in this chapter to evaluate them.

Step 1: Understand the argument.
Skim for the main idea, read with the main idea in mind, identify evidence, and summarize.

Step 2: Seek out competing views and additional evidence.
Critical thinking takes place when all sides of an issue are given a fair hearing.

Step 3: Sort out disagreements.
To overcome confusion, discover where disagreements lie, look at the evidence offered for each view, and construct an overall view.

Step 4: Test the argument for reasonableness.
Check the quantity and quality of the evidence and the soundness of the opinion.

What is an

THE WORD *ARGUMENT* is sometimes used in the sense of "quarrel"—that is, a dispute characterized by angry exchanges. That is not the sense intended here. We will use the term as philosophers do, to mean presenting a point of view about an issue. When you read about opinion and evidence in Chapter One, you were dealing with the essential components of argument. Now consider the longer, more detailed form of argument found in formal writing.

Not all writing can be classified as argument. Novels narrate imaginary incidents in imaginary people's lives to provide the pleasure of vicarious experience. Biographies narrate real incidents in real people's lives to provide similar pleasure, as well as interesting facts. News articles detail current events to enable readers to remain informed about vital or otherwise interesting issues. Argument is different. It does not aim to give pleasure or to inform, though it may on occasion do either or both. Instead, it aims to present a line of thought so clearly and logically that readers are compelled to acknowledge its reasonableness. Simply said, argument aims to persuade.

A quarrel cannot be conducted by one person unless he or she has a split personality. But it takes only one person to engage in argument. Elected officials are arguing when they explain their positions on issues. So are journalists when they write editorials or "opinion pieces," educators when they propose changes in curriculums and courses, and lawyers when they prepare legal briefs.

An argument may be as short as a single sentence or as long as an article or even a book. In any case, an argument expresses a line of reasoning. Think of an argument as a kind of equation, such as *a* plus *b* equals *c*. Whether the argument is sound or unsound depends on what is actually said in the equation. "Twenty plus seventy equals ninety" is sound. On the other hand, "Thirteen plus fourteen equals thirty" is unsound. So is "Roses are red, Irish setters are red, therefore Irish setters are roses."

Logic offers numerous rules for deciding whether an argument is sound or unsound. Those rules are beyond the scope of this book. For now, ask a simpler question: when is an argument persuasive to critical thinkers? Building on Chapter One, we can answer: *when the evidence presented shows the opinion it supports to be more reasonable than competing opinions.* (To make this demonstration, of course, the evidence must be sufficient in quantity and quality.)

The approach detailed in the following pages can help you evaluate the longer arguments you encounter in magazines, journals, and books. It consists of four steps:

Step 1. Understand the argument.
Step 2. Seek out competing views and additional evidence.
Step 3. Sort out disagreements.
Step 4. Test the argument for reasonableness.

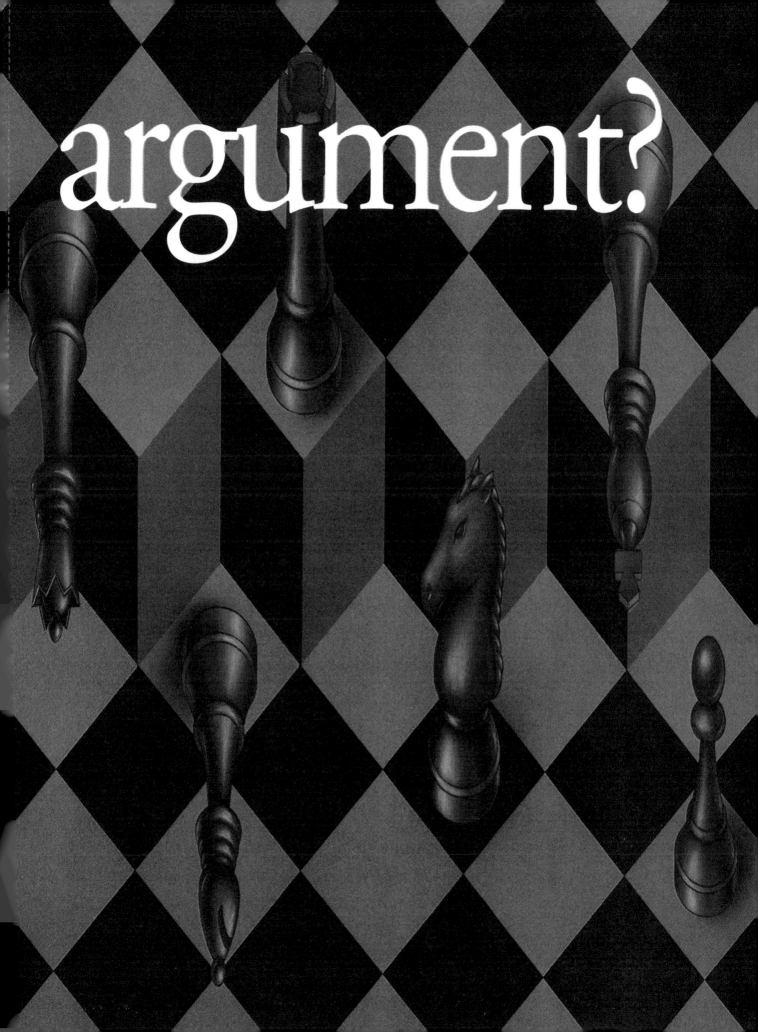

argument?

STEP 1: *Understand the argument*

BRIEF ARGUMENTS are often easily understood. Longer, more detailed arguments pose a greater challenge. In such cases, see the argument as a piece of fabric with many single strands of thought woven together. Closely examine the weave to reveal the individual strands.

Skim for the main idea

To begin, skim the article or book and find the main idea. This idea is usually stated in or immediately after the introduction and is reinforced in the conclusion. The introduction may vary in length. In a brief article, it may be half a paragraph; in a longer article, a paragraph or two; in a book, an entire chapter.

Identifying the main idea is your key to understanding the writer's argument. The writer's choices—what evidence to include, how to arrange it, what objections to address—are made with that idea in mind. If you take time to find the main idea before reading the entire article, reading can be faster and more effective.

Read with the main idea in mind

After skimming the article or book and finding the main idea, read the article or book with the main idea in mind. Distinguish between assertions and evidence. A typical pattern of writers is to make an assertion and then support it with explanation, factual details, examples, and so on. Writers who support their assertions will often include several sentences of support for every sentence of assertion. Not all writers do this, however.

When possible, read the entire article or book in a single sitting. You may find your grasp of the writer's argument improves. To read more efficiently, postpone looking up the definitions of words until later. Of course, if you do not understand a word in the main idea or some other key word, look it up immediately.

Identify evidence

When you finish reading the article or book, look back over it and identify the evidence offered in support of the main idea. Knowing basic relationships between the parts of an argument can help you find evidence quickly and accurately.

"And" relationships signal that what follows adds to what preceded. For example, they may signal that more evidence is being offered to support an assertion. Words used for "and" relationships include *also, first* (*second,* and so on), *in addition, next, further,* and, *moreover, finally, lastly, besides,* and *another.*

"But" relationships signal that what follows *contrasts* with what preceded. What follows is usually an exception or qualification. Words used to signal "but" relationships include *however, nevertheless, yet, or, but, on the other hand,* and *in contrast.*

"Therefore" relationships signal that a conclusion follows from the preceding evidence. Words used to signal "therefore" relationships include *so, consequently, accordingly, thus, therefore,* and *it follows that.*

The illustration below shows the most typical patterns of relationships you'll encounter in persuasive writing and speaking.

Longer articles and books will include a series of these relationships. One example: _____, and _____, and _____, but _____, and _____, therefore_____. (The material represented by each line may comprise a sentence, a paragraph, or a chapter.)

High school English teachers might discourage you from using *and* or *but* to begin a sentence. But that prohibition has no basis. Even a quick scanning of enduring works of literature reveals that writers have used these words to begin sentences. *Therefore,* feel free to do so in your writing. (Notice that this very paragraph is organized in the _____, but _____, therefore_____ pattern.)

As you gain skill in unraveling arguments, you'll be able to identify relationships while you read. For now, treat finding relationships as a separate step.

Summarize

When you have finished reading the article and identifying the evidence offered in support of the main idea, write a summary of the book or article. An effective summary

• Is written in your own words. Using your own words rather than the author's words, helps you remember the ideas.

• Emphasizes key points. Authors use the same techniques taught in high school and college writing. They make assertions, develop them, and present examples. In summarizing, record only the assertions and leave out the supporting material.

• Is accurate. Paraphrasing can cause mistakes. Take care that your summary represents the author's view accurately. If the author emphasizes or qualifies a point, reflect this in your summary. If you wish to add your own comments, put them in brackets. Then you can easily identify them as your own later.

Carefully done summaries can really help you understand arguments in books and articles.

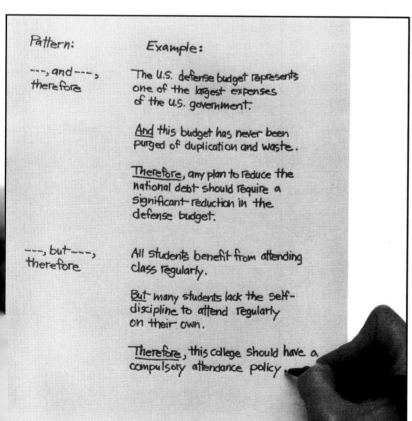

Pattern:

---, and ---, therefore

---, but ---, therefore

Example:

The U.S. defense budget represents one of the largest expenses of the U.S. government.

And this budget has never been purged of duplication and waste.

Therefore, any plan to reduce the national debt should require a significant reduction in the defense budget.

All students benefit from attending class regularly.

But many students lack the self-discipline to attend regularly on their own.

Therefore, this college should have a compulsory attendance policy.

EXERCISE #29

Analyze the arguments in each of the following articles, following the steps explained in "Step 1: Understand the argument." Write your responses in the spaces provided. Future assignments will build on this one.

THE GOVERNMENT'S ROLE IN GAMBLING

The man waits nervously in the long line of people. He's already late for work, and he knows the boss will be angry with him. But he's determined not to leave; he has a strong feeling that this will be the luckiest day of his life. What could possibly be important enough to risk offending one's employer? Buying a ticket on the lottery.

Today's lottery operations and their companion enterprises, off-track betting parlors, are big business. Government officials see them as ideal ways to raise billions of dollars in revenue without raising taxes. The reasoning is that since many people enjoy gambling and no one is hurt by it, there's nothing wrong with the government's taking a piece of the action and using the proceeds to benefit the public.

That reasoning is mistaken. Gambling is a vice. People are hurt by it. It's wrong for the government to be involved in it—every bit as wrong as it would be for the government to run a chain of brothels or a tobacco company or a liquor distillery.

Addiction to gambling is no less a disease than alcoholism. People afflicted by it do not act freely when they place a bet; they are compelled to do so. And they aren't the only ones hurt when they throw away their money: their spouses and children also suffer. Money that could buy food and clothing, pay the rent ,or buy dental care is invested in the childish expectation of beating the odds.

The advertisements for the lottery and off-track betting are cleverly crafted to create the impression that the bettor has a good chance of winning. For example, one commercial begins with the words to an old song, "Fairy tales can come true, it can happen to you . . ." and goes on to dramatize the experience of winning. Slogans like "You can't win it if you're not in it," tease bettors to buy a ticket. And the one in ten or twenty million people who happens to win a big jackpot has his or her picture in the paper and is an instant celebrity, whereas the losers are never mentioned.

If the government used such tactics to tempt alcoholics or smokers, people would be outraged. Rightly so. The government's proper role is to safeguard the people's rights, not to profit from their weakness and gullibility. The fact that the proceeds from gambling are put to good use in no way diminishes the offense of government involvement in it.

State the controlling idea of the article:

_____

_____

_____

_____

_____

_____

Identify relationships among the ideas ("And . . .," "but . . .," and so on):

_____

_____

_____

_____

_____

Summarize the article:

_____

_____

_____

_____

_____

_____

A DAY'S PAY FOR A DAY'S WORK

Every year during football or basketball season, some college in the country makes headlines when one of its athletes is suspended for violating his amateur status by receiving money. Self-righteous windbags around the country then rant on about the importance of protecting college athletics from professionalism and ensuring that athletes place education before sports. Not only is that view hypocritical; it's also absurd. The best thing that could happen to college athletics would be for the myth of amateurism to be exposed and the NCAA to abandon its regulation prohibiting pay for play.

To begin with, college athletes have only one reason for going to college—to get a chance to play professional sports. They couldn't care less about an education. Many of them can't read and write, so the courses they take are just warmed-over junior high school subjects. The idea that their education is going to better their position in life is a cruel deception on them. Few others besides athletes are foolish enough to buy such a notion.

Some people argue that if college athletes were paid for playing sports, they would be corrupted. Surely it wouldn't be any less corrupting than the present situation, in which they receive money under the table and in the process violate ethics and law. And it would spare universities that are supposed to represent society's highest values the embarrassment and shame that accompany unfavorable newspaper headlines.

The only sensible course of action for the N.C.A.A., and for that matter the Olympic Committee, to take is to discard the phony distinction between amateur and professional. Let colleges run their athletic programs as moneymaking ventures (as many of them now do, dishonestly). Allow them to recruit the best players they can without having to enroll them in academic programs. And permit the players to earn salaries and work full-time at their sports. The players will be happier, the teams will perform better, and everyone's conscience will be a lot clearer.

State the controlling idea of the article:

_____

_____

_____

_____

_____

_____

Identify relationships among the ideas (And . . ., but . . ., and so on):

_____

_____

_____

_____

_____

_____

Summarize the article:

_____

_____

_____

_____

_____

_____

A PUBLIC DISSERVICE

Talk-show TV often displays a mindlessness that's as amazing as it is appalling. One Ricki Lake program provides an excellent example (Ricki Lake, NBC–TV, April 5, 1994). It featured several teenagers who had decided to drop out of high school. The program began with the teens presenting their reasons for quitting, then proceeded to have their parents, a guest expert, and the host try to persuade them to stay in school. In the third and final segment the teenagers were given an opportunity to counter the arguments of their elders. No doubt the host and the producers believed they were doing a public service by helping to alleviate the problem of high school dropouts. A moment's reflection will expose the error of that notion.

Being invited to appear on an hour-long nationally syndicated TV show is an honor few people are ever fortunate enough to receive. Most scientists, scholars, inventors, physicians, attorneys, and researchers— people who make significant contributions to the world— never receive such an invitation. Yet those would-be dropouts were so honored. During that hour they became celebrities and their woefully shortsighted rationale for leaving school was dignified. Worse, they were accorded a distinct advantage by being allowed not only the opportunity to explain their decision but also a chance to rebut their elders.

Did Ricki Lake and her producers seriously believe those young people would return to school chastened and enlightened about the importance of formal learning? It's hard to imagine that could happen. After all, their friends and neighbors undoubtedly saw them on TV. And if not, the teens surely have a videotape of the event and will be more than willing to show it, over and over, to document how they held their own in the debate. With a little imagination, they can even expand their delusion and believe a career in television awaits them after they drop out of school! And every child who watched the show will be tempted to see those teens as heroes and regard dropping out of school as a bold assertion of individuality.

In short, this type of program makes the job of parents and teachers more difficult—as if it weren't difficult enough already. Popular culture already has persuaded many young people that they know more than their parents and teachers, that having a right to an opinion means every opinion is right, and that learning is a giant waste of time. Television shows that dignify or reinforce such nonsense can hardly be considered a public service. In reality they're a public disservice.

State the controlling idea of the article:

---

*Identify relationships among the ideas ("And . . . ,"
"but . . . ," and so on):*

Summarize the article:

STEP 2: *Seek out competing views and additional evidence*

COMPETING VIEWS are those that challenge the argument you are evaluating. If you disagree with the argument, you will be strongly motivated to find views that oppose it. But if you agree, you may be tempted to ignore competing views. Resist this temptation.

Critical thinking takes place when all sides of the issue are given a fair hearing. An opposing view may be more insightful than the one you are evaluating. Finding out whether or not that is the case is important. If you are forced to change your own view in the process, that's no reason to be disappointed. You've exchanged a mistaken view for a more valid one. And if thorough investigation supports your view, you've gained valuable insight into why others disagree. These insights can help you construct more persuasive arguments for your view.

Whenever possible, gain firsthand knowledge of the subject in question. For example, if you are evaluating someone's argument that a particular television show is excellent, watch at least a few episodes of the show.

Next, consult authorities on the subject. (Where the subject is not something that can be examined directly, start here.) Not all authorities live far away. Instructors at your school are authorities on their subjects, so consult them. Also remember that several different kinds of expertise may be relevant to your topic. The subject of education, for example, is of interest to sociologists, economists, psychologists, and historians as well as educators. If the professionals you consult don't have the expertise needed for the particular issue you're researching, they will usually be able to direct you to someone who does.

On the rare occasions when you can't find any expertise at your school, use your ingenuity. For a medical issue, call the State Public Health Department or the county medical association. Ask to be referred to an appropriate person in your area. The telephone directory lists the numbers of these and other agencies.

When planning to interview any authority, make an appointment in advance. If you assume the person is available to talk the first time you call, you might not get an interview. State clearly the purpose of the interview and how long you expect it to take.

When it is time for the interview, arrive (or call) on time with questions planned in advance. If the person gives you permission, tape the interview. That way the person won't have to wait while you take notes.

While interviewing, avoid asking questions that can be answered with a simple yes or no. Instead, ask open-ended questions, such as "What do you think about . . . ?" and "What is the basis for your thinking . . . ?" Doing so invites more response from the person you're interviewing. Throughout the interview focus on understanding what the person is saying. Guard against letting your mind wander—for example, to devising counterarguments when you disagree with what is said.

Listen carefully to each answer and ask follow-up questions when appropriate. End the interview on time.

Besides consulting available authorities, you can sample competing views and gain additional evidence by visiting the library and using the following research tools.

Encyclopedias.

Encyclopedias contain articles written by authorities on many subjects. Most articles are brief and highly readable. Where controversy exists, the authors describe it without taking sides. Two good general encyclopedias are *Encyclopedia Americana* and *Encyclopedia Britannica*.

Also, many special encyclopedias cover specific subjects. Examples are encyclopedias on religion and ethics, philosophy, law, medicine, superstition and folklore, and science and technology. These treat their subjects in the same objective fashion but in greater depth than general encyclopedias.

Almanacs.

Almanacs provide miscellaneous facts and statistics about a wide range of subjects. Most are published annually. The *World Almanac* is available from 1868 to the present.

Periodical indexes.

These reference books will guide you to magazine, journal, and newspaper articles on your subject. The index to consult for general magazines is the *Reader's Guide to Periodical Literature*. For scholarly journals, consult more specialized indexes. Examples are the *Humanities Index*, the *Social Science Index*, and the *Business Periodicals Index*. The *New York Times Index* covers every article written in that newspaper since 1851. Your library may have the entire collection on microfilm.

Abstract publications.

These reference books are especially helpful, offering summaries of articles and books. Many abstract publications arc available, including *Psychological Abstracts* and *Research in Education*.

Government publications.

The U.S. government is the largest publisher in the world. Consult *The Monthly Guide to U.S. Publications* for available materials.

Computer databases.

Modern technology makes data searches easy. Inquire about the databases available in your library.

The library catalog.

This catalog, in most cases computerized, is your library's way of keeping track of all its holdings. It is arranged in three ways: by subject, author, and title.

The library staff.

The most important resource in any library is the people who work there. Your librarians can help you find the research tools listed here and suggest others. If you were researching a current issue, they might direct you to *Facts on File*, a weekly news digest. Or they might suggest *Editorials on File*, a biweekly collection of newspaper editorials from around the United States and Canada.

Before ending your research, be sure you've taken a fair sampling of the range of views on the issue. Also check that your statistical data is up-to-date.

EXERCISE #30

Select one of your responses to Exercise #29. Seek competing views and additional evidence, using appropriate research sources from the list presented above. Record your findings on a separate sheet of paper. (Future assignments will build on this one.)

STEP 3: *Sort out disagreements*

WHEN YOU CONSULT AUTHORITIES, you may find that they all agree on an issue. In that case, you can summarize their common view and decide whether or not it is the most reasonable one.

More often, though, you'll find that authorities disagree on certain aspects of the issue—or the entire issue. If there are a number of aspects, you may be confused about how to sort out and appraise the disagreements.

To overcome confusion, deal with one aspect at a time. You can begin by making a spreadsheet. Just put the names of the authorities across the top of the page and list the aspects down the left side. Then indicate each authority's view on each aspect. If you consult more than a few authorities, you may have to tape two or three more sheets side by side.

Suppose you're investigating the issue "Should boxing be outlawed?" The photo on this page shows how your spreadsheet might look.

	MEDICAL DOCTOR	FORMER BOXER	SPORTS JOURNALIST	CRITIC OF BOXING
Is boxing a sport?	No	Yes	Yes	No
Is the intention in boxing to injure the opponent?	Yes	Yes	No	Yes
Is boxing dangerous?	Yes	Yes	Yes	Yes
Can the risk of injury be overcome by training?	No	Yes	Yes	No
Can the risk of injury be overcome by protective gear?	No	No	Yes	No
Would outlawing boxing deny minorities a way out of poverty?	No	Yes	Yes	

Next, look across each aspect of the issue and find where the disagreements lie. With the boxing issue, our spreadsheet shows no disagreement on the danger. It shows some disagreement on the aspect of intentional harm, and considerable disagreement on the other four aspects.

When you find a disagreement, look back at the evidence offered for each view. Then you can decide which authority makes the most persuasive case for that aspect. At this point it helps to consult your own experience. When you're thinking critically, don't assume any authority is right on every aspect of an issue.

Your decisions on the various aspects of the issue will give you an overall view of the issue. Since some aspects will be more important than others, your overall view will seldom be a mere sum of your decisions. You may agree with one person's view on several aspects of the issue, yet disagree with her overall view. Here's how your overall view of the boxing issue might look:

> *Boxing is not properly classified as a sport because the contestants intend to injure each other. When injuries occur in other sports, they occur accidentally or when rules are broken. As a result, boxing is dangerous. It's true that training and protective gear can reduce the threat to fighters but not eliminate it. For these reasons, I believe boxing should be outlawed. I admit that such action would deny members of minority groups one way of rising above poverty, but better ways can and should be created.*

Developed in a composition, this view would be more detailed. You would present each point, state the authorities you consulted, and support your overall view.

EXERCISE #31

On a separate sheet, make a spreadsheet for the issue you investigated in Exercise #30. Follow the directions and the example on the topic of boxing, shown on the previous page. Future assignments will build on this one.

STEP 4: *Test the argument for reasonableness*

AN ARGUMENT IS persuasive to skilled thinkers when the evidence presented demonstrates that the opinion it supports is more reasonable than competing opinions. To make this demonstration, the evidence must be sufficient in quantity and quality. Step 4 is about deciding whether an argument meets this criterion.

We make this decision by using two broad kinds of testing. One concerns the evidence and the other concerns the opinion itself.

Testing evidence

We may thoroughly seek out additional evidence, and we may add our own findings to the some-times considerable evidence that authors present. Even so, our data may be incomplete. Getting *all* the evidence relevant to a question is at best difficult. Given this fact, we may wonder what "evidence sufficient in quantity and quality" means and how we can decide when it has been achieved.

Evidence is sufficient in quality when it is relevant to the issue and is accurately presented. For example, consider the statement "Women comprise only 2.8 percent of the workers in this field." This statement would be sufficient in quality if (a) this statistic had a bearing on the matter being addressed and (b) the percentage was indeed 2.8, not 2.9 or 4.6.

Deciding when the *quantity* of evidence is sufficient is more difficult. The answer depends on how sweeping the opinion is. If the opinion were "A relationship *may exist* between disrespect of elders and poor grades in school," a single reputable study would be sufficient evidence.

Suppose the wording were slightly changed: "A relationship exists between disrespect of elders and poor grades in school." Now the demand for evidence is greatly increased. The person advancing this argument would have to demonstrate that (a) all relevant research studies have produced this conclusion or (b) most studies have and those that did not were flawed. And if the opinion were stated even more ambitiously—"Disrespect of elders causes young people to have poor grades in school"—the demand for evidence would be even greater.

When the evidence offered in support of an opinion is inadequate, the argument is obviously not persuasive. But this does not necessarily mean that the opinion at the heart of the argument is mistaken. Other evidence may exist, sufficient in quantity and quality to support the opinion. Carelessness or some other reason may have prevented the author from discovering it.

Testing opinions

Chapter One explains four ways to test opinions for reasonableness. Now review those ways and then look at some new ones.

1. *Think of situations in which the opinion ought to apply and decide whether it does apply.* When testing the opinion that truth is relative, we considered a variety of situations. Among them were Galileo's conclusion that the earth revolves around the sun, the duties of a jury, and the existence of concentration camps.

2. *Think of exceptions to the claim set forth in the opinion.* To test the opinion "You are the only thing that is real. Everything else is your imagination," we considered some things outside ourselves that are nevertheless very real.

3. *Check relevant research to see if it supports the opinion.* To test the opinion that a child of two can know better than her mother what's good for her, you were invited to check research in child psychology.

4. *Search out competing opinions to determine whether any of them are more reasonable than the opinion in question.* This approach was explained in an earlier section of this chapter, "Seek out competing views and additional evidence."

Following are additional ways to test an opinion.

5. *If the author offers an example, think of counterexamples.*

Example:
I know a person who was given responsibilities such as picking up his clothes and toys at age three, taking out the garbage at age six, and raking leaves, washing dishes, and doing laundry by age ten. Today he's in his mid-thirties and he resents having had all those chores. To top it off, he's not a very reliable worker today. [This example is offered in support of the argument "Children should not be given responsibilities around the house until they are in their mid-teens."]

Counterexample:
Consult your memory. Think of an adult (perhaps yourself) who had such responsibilities and yet regards the experience as valuable.

6. *Reverse the opinion.* That is, take the exact opposite view and make a case for it.

The opinion:
People must feel good about themselves before they can achieve in school or in life. [This idea, many readers will recognize, is a tenet of the self-esteem movement.]

The test:
Reverse the opinion to "People must achieve in school or in life before they can feel good about themselves." Your case might include examples of how achievement builds confidence, even at an early age. Examples include a child learning to eat with a spoon, walk, tie shoelaces, ride a bike, and read.

7. *Consider the implications of the opinion.* Think about how accepting the opinion affects other ideas. Finding negative implications can help you see flaws you might otherwise miss.

The opinion:
What people view in movies or on television has no effect on their behavior. [Media spokespeople often say this in response to complaints that graphic sex and violence have a negative social impact.]

The implications:
Viewing films and television produces neither positive effects nor negative effects. So, film and television cannot degrade us or inspire and motivate us to buy new products. If that is really the case, then public service announcements to drive sober and practice safer sex are pointless and advertisers waste billions of dollars.

8. Consider the consequences that have occurred or are likely to occur if the idea is put into practice.

The opinion:
The welfare system that continues to drain our tax dollars should be not gradually phased out but ended immediately.

The consequences:
Some able-bodied welfare recipients would seek work and find it. Others would be less successful. Those who are too old or too ill to work would be left with no source of income, and the living conditions for welfare children would sharply decline. Private agencies such as the Salvation Army would increase their giving to the extent possible, yet their help might not meet the need.

Not all of these tests fit every opinion. Decide which ones fit the particular opinion you are evaluating. Your test findings will vary. Sometimes they will support the opinion in question. At other times, they will reveal the opinion's weakness and help you construct a more reasonable view. In this case you can combine insights from various viewpoints, as the following example illustrates.

Original argument:
Women's athletic teams at your school should not receive an equal share of the sports budget because men's teams play a more competitive schedule and draw larger crowds at athletic contests.

Significant findings of your research:
1) In the past, the budget was determined first and the teams' schedules were set accordingly. Women were forced to play less competitive schedules because the budget would not permit them to travel far.

2) The attendance at women's athletic events has tripled over the last five years. It's now 65 percent of men's teams' attendance, despite the "softer" schedule.
3) Courts would likely regard the present athletic budget as a form of discrimination against women students.
4) If the budget were divided equally next year, the men's program could not be maintained at its present level.

Revised view:
Women's teams should get an increasing share of the athletic budget each year for the next three years. After three years, their share should be equal to that received by the men's teams. By gradually increasing the women's share, the school can maintain the men's athletic program at its present level while the budget is worked out. Perhaps additional sources of support for both programs can be found.

In all your evaluative work, it is vital that you accept the limits of analysis. Only rarely can we be certain that one view of an issue is correct. More often, the best we can achieve is probability. That is, we can show that one view is more reasonable than others and more likely to be valid. In some cases, all we have are a number of possibilities, all supported by the evidence, but no one more than the others. In these situations, withhold judgment until more evidence is available.

EXERCISE #32
In Exercise #29 (page 64) you began an analysis that continued through Exercises #30 and #31. Now complete that analysis by testing the argument for reasonableness, as explained in "Step 4: Test the argument for reasonableness." Write your response on a separate sheet of paper.

Exercise #33

Read the three arguments that follow. Then choose <u>one</u> argument and apply the four-step approach explained in this chapter. Record the results of your testing in the space provided. Then, on a separate sheet of paper, write a composition of at least three paragraphs discussing the strengths and weaknesses of the original passage. Present what you find to be the most reasonable view of the issue. (You may wish to consult the article "Writing persuasive compositions" in Chapter Five.)

Argument 1:

It's no wonder that crime is out of control in this society and honest citizens live in fear. The prison system is no longer a deterrent to crime. In some cases it almost encourages crime. Inmates are given excellent food and comfortable cells furnished with cable television. Their medical and dental needs are provided for without cost. Prisoners can use library and exercise facilities.

Often inmates do no hard labor in exchange for these benefits. They're free to relax and enjoy themselves while taxpayers toil to pay the bill.

The situation is not only absurd but intolerable. Since the rehabilitation approach doesn't work, prisons should punish criminals. And the first step is to end the country club atmosphere. Remove all the comforts. If we make the prison experience miserable, people will think not once but several times before committing a crime.

Argument 2:

Should editors of college newspapers be allowed to make all their own decisions? Some people say yes. By making decisions, they reason, editors learn a sense of responsibility. This argument overlooks the harm a careless decision can do.

If an editor decides to publish a story with a racist message, every minority student on campus will be insulted and outraged. If the editor publishes a defense of male chauvinism, every woman on campus will feel wronged. If the editor publishes a story that mocks religion, every religious student will be offended. In all three cases, the newspaper encourages the very intolerance that education is supposed to conquer.

Editors of college newspapers are not professional journalists. They're merely students learning another subject, in this case journalism. Therefore, they should not be allowed to make important editorial decisions. Such decisions should be made by faculty advisors.

Argument 3:

Recently the faculty of a school district in a northeastern state voted unanimously to reject merit pay awards. The faculty did not object to the amount of the awards. They objected to the very idea of determining who the best teachers are and giving them, in effect, a bonus for excellence.

The faculty in that school district acted wisely and courageously. It does not matter how the selection is made; selecting some faculty for merit awards implies that others are not as deserving. That implication hurts feelings, creates dissension, and undermines faculty morale. In the long run it results in poorer education for students.

Whenever a school board has money to give faculty, it should be divided among all teachers. That would convey an encouraging message to teachers: "You're all doing an excellent job."

Your testing:

_____

_____

_____

_____

_____

_____

_____

_____

_____

_____

_____

_____

_____

_____

_____

_____

_____

Exercise #34

Read both of the arguments below. Then choose <u>one</u> argument and apply the four-step approach explained in this chapter. Record the results of your testing in the space provided. Then, on a separate sheet of paper, write a composition of at least three paragraphs discussing the strengths and weaknesses of the original passage. Present what you find to be the most reasonable view of the issue. (You may wish to consult the article "Expressing your ideas persuasively" in Chapter Five.)

Argument 1:
The headline screams "Binge Drinking Soars Among College Women." Increasing numbers of college women, it seems, purposely drink to get drunk. And being drunk makes them more vulnerable to casual sex, pregnancy, and sexually transmitted diseases, including AIDS, not to mention rape. The amazing thing is not the report itself but the response of many journalists and social analysts, who wring their collective hands, scratch their collective heads and ask why, what can possibly explain this development.

The answer may elude these professionals, but it's clear enough to many less sophisticated Americans. Youthful binge drinkers are simply following the advice they've received from the media all their lives. Reebok counsels them, "Life is short—play hard." Nike sells them T-shirts that advise "Just do it." Psychologists tell them, "Whatever feels good is good; follow your feelings." Anyone who is surprised that ideas have consequences needs a remedial course in reality.

Common sense suggests that politically correct agonizing doesn't solve problems. Journalists and commentators would do well to examine everyday events for the root causes of America's social problems. In the case of binge drinking, they should consider the sorry advertising practice of using irresponsible appeals to sell products.

Argument 2:
TV and movie apologists are forever telling us that we have no business criticizing them because they are only holding a mirror up to reality. Many people buy that explanation, but they shouldn't. It would be more accurate to say the media hold a magnifying glass to carefully selected realities—namely, the most outrageous and sensational events of the day. The cases of Joey Buttafuoco, Tonya Harding, Michael Jackson, the Menendez brothers, and Lorena Bobbitt come to mind.

Consider how this happens. The first platoon of media people report the latest sensational story as it unfolds, squeezing each new development for all the airtime or newsprint it will yield. Meanwhile, agents and attorneys are negotiating the sale of movie and TV rights to the story. The sleazier the story, the greater the payoff. After the movie is produced, every situation comedy, detective show, and western drama builds a show around the successful theme. So a single despicable, disgusting act in real life—real or imagined—can generate months of sensational media fare.

In short, the media exploit our social problems for ratings, feed us a steady diet of debasing material, celebrate irresponsible behavior, and then have the audacity to blame parents and teachers for the social problems that result.

Your testing:

_____
_____
_____
_____
_____
_____
_____
_____
_____
_____
_____
_____
_____
_____
_____
_____
_____
_____
_____
_____

PRACTICING CRITICAL THINKING #10

Look back at the list of observations you prepared in response to Practicing Critical Thinking #9 in Chapter Two. Select one of those observations, restate it below, and then add your reflections, as explained in Chapter One. Observations, remember, are interesting issues, statements that appear insightful (or mistaken), probing questions, ideas that may have wider implications, or anything else that you wish to understand more fully, such as an incident, a process, or a procedure. Reflections are your thoughtful analysis of the observations.

Observation

_____
_____
_____
_____
_____
_____

Reflection

_____
_____
_____
_____
_____
_____
_____
_____

PRACTICING CRITICAL THINKING #11

List below any observations you made since you completed your response to Practicing Critical Thinking #9 in Chapter Two. (Note: this Exercise will be repeated at the end of every subsequent chapter. Record any observations that you make between chapters in the following chapter.)

Interesting issues you would like to address when you have more time:

_____
_____
_____
_____
_____
_____

Statements that appear to be unusually insightful. (They may have been made by authors, instructors, fellow students, or anyone else.)

_____
_____
_____
_____
_____

PRACTICING CRITICAL THINKING #11 (CONTINUED)

Statements that seem to be shallow or mistaken. Choose a statement serious enough that you want to know more about its flaws and perhaps respond to them.

_____

_____

_____

_____

_____

_____

_____

Questions that have arisen from your reading or listening or have otherwise occurred to you and seem worth pursuing.

_____

_____

_____

_____

_____

_____

_____

Ideas or situations that seem to have wider implications.

_____

_____

_____

_____

_____

_____

_____

Anything you have experienced or heard about—for example, an incident, a process, or a procedure—that you wish to understand more fully.

_____

_____

_____

_____

_____

_____

_____

Name_____Date____/____/____

1 *Would it be accurate to define an argument as a dispute characterized by angry exchanges? Explain your answer.*

2 *Not all writing presents arguments. True or false? Explain your answer.*

3 *When is an argument persuasive to critical thinkers?*

4 *According to this chapter, the first step in evaluating a longer argument is understanding the argument. What are the other three steps?*

5 *Explain the approach this chapter presents for understanding an argument.*

6 *What are features of an effective summary?*

QUIZ

CONTINUED

7 *What are open-ended questions, and when does this chapter suggest that you use them?*

8 *What is the most important resource available in any library?*

9 *When you consult authorities and find that they disagree about an issue, you may become confused. What tip does this chapter offer for overcoming such confusion?*

10 *When the evidence offered in support of an opinion is inadequate, you can be certain the opinion is mistaken. True or false? Explain your answer.*

11 *This chapter added several new ways to test opinions for reasonableness to the ways presented in Chapter One. What are those new ways?*

4.
Recognizing Errors in Thinking

Three kinds of errors.
Be alert for errors of perception, judgment, and reaction.

Errors of perception.
Errors often begin in faulty ways of seeing the world—"mine is better" thinking, selective perception, gullibility, skepticism, bias, pretending to know, and either/or thinking.

Errors of judgment.
Double standards, irrelevant criteria, overgeneralizing, stereotyping, hasty conclusions, assumptions, failure to make distinctions, and oversimplifying are the main kinds of judgment errors.

Errors of reaction.
When we explain away ideas, shift the burden of proof, attack the person, or set up a "straw man," we risk fooling ourselves.

Errors can multiply.
Any error in thinking invites more.

3 KINDS OF ERRORS

*Most often people seek in life occasions for persisting
in their opinions rather than for educating themselves.
Each of us looks for justification in the event.
The rest, which runs counter to that opinion,
is overlooked. . . . It seems as if the mind enjoys
nothing more than sinking deeper into error.*

André Gide

PERHAPS GIDE OVERSTATED THE PROBLEM in
suggesting that we *enjoy* error. But he was
wise in noting our difficulty in dealing with
issues objectively and logically. To overcome that
difficulty, we need to understand the kinds of
errors that can entrap us and the steps we can
take to avoid them.

Three broad types of errors are common:
errors of perception, errors of judgment, and
errors of reaction.

ERRORS OF PERCEPTION

Errors of perception are not blunders made while examining issues. They are faulty ways of seeing reality, preventing us from being open-minded even before we begin to apply our critical thinking. The following are especially serious.

"Mine is better" thinking

As small children we may have said, "My mommy is prettier than any other mommy" or "My daddy is bigger and stronger." Perhaps we had similar thoughts about our houses, toys, and finger paintings.

Now that we've gotten older, we probably don't express "mine is better" thinking. Yet we may still indulge in it. Such thinking often occurs in matters that are important to us, such as our race, religion, ethnic group, social class, political party, or philosophy of life.

This habit is not always obvious. In fact, "mine is better" thinking can be quite subtle. We may be quite uninterested in a person until we find out she is Irish, like us. Suddenly we feel a sense of kinship. We may think a person is rather dense until he says something that matches our view. Then we decide he's really quite bright after all.

"Mine is better" thinking is natural and often harmless. Even so, this kind of thinking creates distance between people through a win-lose mentality. This can easily prevent you from learning from others. To prevent this, remember that opening your mind to ideas from other people can broaden your perspective and lead to fresh insights. Give every idea a fair hearing—even an idea that challenges your own.

Selective perception

In one sense, we see selectively most of the time. Let's say you and two friends, a horticulture major and an art major, walk through a shopping mall. You want to buy a pair of shoes; the others are just taking a break from studying. The same reality exists for each of you: stores, potted plants, people passing by. Still, each of you focuses on different things. While you are looking for shoe stores, one friend notices the plants. The other studies faces for interesting features.

Later, one of you says, "Hey, did you see the big new store in the mall?" The others say no. Though the store was before all of your eyes, two of you screened it out.

That kind of selective perception is often harmless. Another kind of selective perception takes place when we focus on things that support our current ideas and reject anything that challenges them. Suppose someone thinks that a particular ethnic group is stupid, violent, cheap, or lazy. Then "stupid" behaviors will capture that person's attention. And if his bias is strong enough, he will completely miss intelligent behaviors from members of that group. He'll only see evidence that supports his prejudice.

You can break the habit of selective perception by looking and listening for details you haven't seen before. Also press yourself to balance your perception. If you find yourself focusing on negative details, look for positive ones, and vice versa.

Gullibility and skepticism

Philosopher Alfred Korzybski observed, "there are two ways to slide easily through life: to believe everything or to doubt everything—both ways save us from thinking." To believe everything we are told is to be gullible. To doubt everything is to be skeptical.

An alternative to gullibility and skepticism is questioning. This means greeting all ideas with curiosity and wonder, judging none of them in advance, and being equally prepared to find wisdom, foolishness, or some combination of the two.

Bias toward the majority or the minority

Bias tends to follow our affections. If we feel more comfortable with the majority on our side, we may choose the majority view. If we identify with the underdog and love the challenge of confronting superior numbers, we may embrace the minority view.

Each of these choices can occur with little or no awareness of our underlying bias. And in each case we put feelings of comfort and personal preference above the evidence. Critical thinking means deciding issues on their merits rather than on the number or the celebrity status of the people on the opposing sides.

Pretending to know

Some people believe that confessing ignorance makes them look ineffective, so they pretend to know things they really don't. After a while, pretending becomes a habit that hinders critical thinking. Suppose someone says on several occasions, "I've read quite a few books on psychology." Also suppose the truth is different and he's never read a book on the subject. The idea will become so familiar that he might take it for the truth. What's more, he'll begin to confuse his guesses about psychology with real knowledge. Practice staying aware of your statements and remaining alert for pretense. Whenever you find it, acknowledge the truth and resolve not to lie to yourself or others again.

Bias for or against change

According to an old joke, conservatives have never met a new idea they liked, and liberals have never met a new idea they didn't like. Each observation contains an element of truth.

Some people find even small changes, like returning home and finding the furniture rearranged, very upsetting. Major changes, like moving across the country, can be even more disturbing.

New ideas can have a similar effect on such people. Old beliefs provide a sense of comfort and security. When those beliefs are challenged, people may feel that reality has been pulled out from under them. That's probably why ancient rulers killed the bearers of bad news. It's also one reason why persuading others can be difficult.

Bias against change may be older and more common than bias for change. Yet the latter seems to be increasing today, perhaps because technology is advancing so rapidly. Some people think that old ideas, old beliefs, old values are of little value today. For them, new is always better.

Neither perspective is consistent with critical thinking. Some new ideas are clearly better than the old ones they replace. Progress has in fact occurred in every area of life, including science, technology, education, and government. Yet this reality has another, less fortunate side. New ideas sometimes contain serious flaws that go unnoticed at first. Time and experience sometimes prove that the supposed great leap forward was actually several steps backward.

To avoid bias for or against change, know your own mental habits. Also be alert for bias in your thinking.

Either/or thinking

This error of perception means taking only extreme positions on an issue when other positions are possible.

For example, one person thinks that accepting evolution means rejecting the idea of Creation. Another person thinks that being Republican means taking a conservative stance on every issue.

Yet it's possible to believe in evolution and Creation. You could believe that God created the universe and planned it to evolve over millions of years. You could also be a Republican without always taking a conservative stand.

Either/or thinking hampers critical thinking. This error forces us to take extreme, unreasonable views. To avoid either/or thinking, look for times when there seem to be only two possible views. Ask yourself, Are these the only possibilities? Could another view be more reasonable— perhaps one that includes elements of both?

An example is the debate over crime prevention. Some elected officials argue for banning assault weapons and registering handguns. The National Rifle Association argues for getting criminals off the street. You might ask, Why not take both actions and add others, such as building more prisons, as well?

EXERCISE #35

Consider each of the seven errors of perception. Think of a time when you've committed each one and describe these situations. Explain how you reacted and what consequences followed. Then decide how you might have avoided the error and how the consequences could have been different.

"Mine is better" thinking

_____

_____

_____

_____

_____

_____

Selective perception

_____

_____

_____

_____

_____

_____

Gullibility and skepticism

_____

_____

_____

_____

_____

_____

Bias toward the majority or the minority

_____

_____

_____

_____

_____

Pretending to know

_____

_____

_____

_____

_____

_____

_____

_____

Bias for or against change

_____

_____

_____

_____

_____

_____

Either/or thinking

_____

_____

_____

_____

_____

_____

ERRORS OF JUDGMENT

Errors of judgment occur in the process of sorting out and assessing evidence. Look for the following.

Double standard

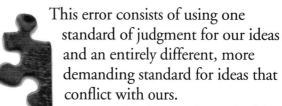

This error consists of using one standard of judgment for our ideas and an entirely different, more demanding standard for ideas that conflict with ours.

People who employ a double standard ignore inconsistencies, contradictions, and outrageous overstatements in arguments they agree with. Yet they nitpick their opponents' arguments. They even use different vocabularies. Allies are described as "imaginative," "forceful," and "brutally honest." Opponents with the same qualities are labeled "utopian," "belligerent," or "mean-spirited."

Critical thinking demands a single standard of judgment for those who agree with us and for those who disagree.

Irrelevant criterion

This error consists of criticizing an idea because it fails to do what it wasn't intended to do. Say that a chief executive proposes a new reward program for employees' cost-saving ideas in his company. Supervisors argue against the program because it doesn't increase the percentage of women and minorities in the company. In this case, the supervisors are invoking an irrelevant criterion.

The point is not that fairness to women and minorities is unimportant. Rather, fairness is a different issue and should not be made the measure of the reward program.

You can avoid the mistake of using irrelevant criteria. When you evaluate an idea, set aside all separate issues and agendas, no matter how important they are or how committed you feel about them.

Overgeneralizing or stereotyping

Generalizations are judgments about a class of people or things. Political pollsters are generalizing when they say, "Most voters don't care much about either presidential candidate." Though such a statement covers tens of millions of people, it's a fair one if based on a representative sample of those people.

Generalizations don't have to be based on a scientific sampling in order to be fair. They need only be based on a reasonable number of contacts with a reasonable number of people in the group. For example, your instructor might say, "My present students are more willing to participate in class than my students were last year." Or you could say, "The people in my neighborhood are friendly."

Overgeneralizations are unfair generalizations. They exceed what's appropriate to conclude from our experiences. Suppose a professor teaches only advanced French literature and sees only a small, unique group of students. If she says something about "the students at this college" based solely on her experience, she is thinking uncritically. Or consider a first semester student who has contact with only five teachers. This person would be overgeneralizing if he judged "the faculty at this school."

Stereotypes are overgeneralizations that harden into convictions shared by many people. There are stereotypes of people: fundamentalists, politicians, feminists, psychiatrists, rock musicians. And there are stereotypes of places and things: New York City and San Francisco, marriage and farming.

Overgeneralizations and stereotypes hinder critical thinking by blinding us to important differences among individual people, places, and things.

Hasty conclusion

Hasty conclusions are conclusions drawn without enough evidence. Consider this case: A college student often leaves his dorm room open and many people have access to it. One day he discovers an expensive pen is missing from his desk. He concludes that his roommate took it. This is a hasty conclusion. It's possible that his roommate stole the pen. It's also possible that someone else stole it. Or perhaps the pen was lost or misplaced.

In many cases, two or more conclusions are possible. Critical thinking means having a good reason for choosing one over the others. If no such reason exists, suspend judgment and seek more evidence.

Unwarranted assumption

Assumptions are ideas we take for granted. They differ from conclusions in an important way: we make assumptions unconsciously. They're implied rather than expressed.

There's nothing necessarily wrong with assumptions. Making them allows us to conduct our daily activities efficiently. When you got up this morning, you assumed there would be enough hot water to take a shower. If you drove to school, you probably assumed that your car would start and your instructors would hold classes. Unless there was a good reason not to make these assumptions—for example, if your water heater was broken—they would be valid.

The assumptions that hinder critical thinking are unwarranted assumptions. These occur when we take too much for granted. When this happens, we're prevented from asking useful questions and exploring possibilities.

Suppose someone assumes that it's the teacher's job to make a class interesting. That person is unlikely to ask herself, What responsibility do the *students* have to create interesting classes? That omission results from her unwarranted assumption. Below is an excerpt from a student conversation:

Sally: You say that discrimination against women is a thing of the past. That's just not true.

Ralph: It certainly is true. I read it in a magazine.

Ralph has made a common unwarranted assumption: if something appears in print, it must be true. Notice that he hasn't said this. He may not even realize he's making any assumption. Nevertheless, he clearly implies it.

The fact that assumptions are unstated makes them hard to detect. When you look for assumptions in your own thinking and writing, go beyond what you consciously thought or wrote. Consider what you took for granted.

Failure to make a distinction

Distinctions are subtle differences among things. Care in making distinctions can help you overcome confusion and deal with complex issues effectively. Following are some important distinctions to recognize.

The distinction between the person and the idea. Critical thinkers judge an idea on its own merits—not on the celebrity status or expertise of the person expressing it. Though experts usually have more informed views than novices, experts can be wrong and novices can have genuine insights.

The distinction between assertion and evidence. Some people pile assertion upon assertion without evidence. If these people are articulate, the casual thinker may be persuaded. Critical thinkers judge ideas on how well supported—and supportable—they are. This is more important than how well the idea is expressed.

The distinction between familiarity and validity. We're naturally attracted to the familiar. It's easy to believe that reasoning is valid merely because we've heard it many times. Critical thinkers are not swayed by familiarity.

The distinction between often *and* always, seldom, *and* never. Uncritical thinkers tend to ignore this distinction. They might say something "always" occurs when the evidence supports only "often," or they might say it "never" occurs when the evidence supports only "seldom." Critical thinkers are careful to make the distinction.

Oversimplification

There's nothing wrong with simplifying. In elementary school especially, teachers simplify their subjects. Professionals such as engineers and chemists simplify to communicate with people untrained in their fields.

Oversimplification differs from simplification. Oversimplification omits essential information or ignores complexity. Consider this idea: "High school teachers have it made. They're through at three o'clock every day and work only nine months of the year." Though there is some truth to this statement, it's inaccurate. Teachers often prepare four or five classes a day, grade homework, keep records, chaperone activities, and advise organizations. These activities often occur outside the normal eight-hour day. In addition, teachers are often required to take summer courses.

Oversimplification distorts reality and confuses discussion.

EXERCISE #36

Consider each of the seven errors of judgment. Think of times when you've committed them, and describe these situations. Explain how you reacted and what events followed. Then decide how you could have avoided the error and how the consequences might have been different.

Double standard

_____

_____

_____

_____

_____

Irrelevant criterion

_____

_____

_____

_____

_____

_____

Overgeneralization or stereotyping

_____

_____

_____

_____

_____

Hasty conclusion

_____

_____

_____

_____

_____

_____

Unwarranted assumption

_____

_____

_____

_____

_____

_____

Failure to make a distinction

_____

_____

_____

_____

_____

Oversimplification

_____

_____

_____

_____

_____

EXERCISE #37

Read each of the following passages carefully, looking for errors of judgment. When you find one, explain what the error is in the space provided .

A.

Sue: My English instructor makes us rewrite any composition that contains more than three errors in grammar or usage. And she's always demanding that we do better in our writing. I think she dislikes us.

Ellen: I know what you mean. The professors at this college seem to think it's Harvard.

_____
_____
_____
_____
_____
_____

B.

Morris: Did you notice all the people using food stamps in the grocery store this morning?

Olaf: Yeah. It seems everybody has them these days. It's the fashionable thing to plead poverty.

Morris: That one woman was dressed well, too. I'll bet her lazy husband was waiting for her outside in a big fancy car.

Olaf: It makes me sick, people like that leeching on society. Darwin had the right idea: survival of the fittest. If people can't survive on their own, let 'em suffer.

_____
_____
_____
_____
_____
_____
_____

C.

Times change, and values in one age are different from values in another. Parents fail to realize this. That's why they keep harping about avoiding alcohol and drugs and postponing sexual involvement. They think that what was right for them is right for us.

_____
_____
_____
_____
_____
_____
_____
_____

D.

Boris: Can you believe the price of textbooks? The average amount I spent for a book this semester was $25, and a good half of my books are paperbacks.

Elaine: Everybody's complaining about it. When the cost of books keeps going up and up, there's only one explanation: the authors and publishers are getting greedy.

Boris: Yeah, and you know one of my instructors has the nerve to make us buy a book he wrote. And get this: He teaches Ethics!

Elaine: Wow.

_____
_____
_____
_____
_____
_____
_____

ERRORS OF REACTION

Errors of reaction occur when you express a viewpoint and someone reacts negatively. They are defensive reactions that preserve your self-image and provide an excuse to maintain your view. The following errors of reaction are the most common.

Explaining away

Ron has been a marijuana smoker for several years. He maintains that marijuana is harmless. Last night he and a group of friends were talking, and one of them mentioned that his health instructor distributed an article from the *Journal of the American Medical Association.*

That article reported the results of a clinical study of marijuana use. It concluded that "contrary to what is frequently reported, we have found the effect of marijuana to be not merely that of a mild intoxicant which causes a slight exaggeration of usual adolescent behavior, but a specific and separate clinical syndrome." The main effects the study noted were "disturbed awareness of the self, apathy, confusion and poor reality testing."

Ron's reply was heated. "Those articles are written by a bunch of pansies who never smoked a joint. They're guessing, fantasizing, or worse, making up scare stories for parents to feed their kiddies. I've smoked pot for years, and I can tell you it's had no effect on me."

Ron found the prospect of being wrong about marijuana and the possibility of injuring himself too unpleasant to consider. This is understandable. Still, critical thinking suggests that he should at least read the article and examine the evidence. Instead, he resorted to a tactic long used in uncritical thinking: explain it away.

When people explain away challenges to their ideas, they don't change reality. They just postpone dealing with it. The longer they postpone, the more painful the experience. If you wish to avoid such results, face unpleasant ideas directly and honestly.

Shifting the burden of proof

Accepting the burden of proof means supporting our assertions. The more the assertions challenge accepted wisdom, the greater the burden. What's more, this burden falls on the person who makes the assertion. Here's how this concept applies in an actual case. Two students are discussing greatness in boxing:

Zeke: Mike Tyson was the greatest heavyweight boxer of all time.

Brad: Wait a minute. There have been a lot of great heavyweights over the years. I doubt Tyson was better than all of them.

Zeke: I stand by my position. Prove me wrong if you can.

There would be nothing wrong with Zeke's asking Brad why he doubts Tyson's greatness. But when Zeke says "Prove me wrong," he's shifting the burden of proof. Since Zeke made the original statement, he should be prepared to defend it.

When you make an assertion, you might be called on to defend it. And if you find that you can't defend an assertion, avoid shifting the burden of proof. Withdraw the assertion.

Attacking the person

In uncritical thinking, there's a common way of reacting to challenges: attack the challenger. Here's a common scenario.

Melissa argues that it makes no sense for students to vote while they're away at college. The process of obtaining an absentee ballot is time-consuming, she says. And with so many people voting, a student's vote isn't that important.

Agnes challenges Melissa's view. "I voted by absentee ballot last year," she says, "and the process was simple." Agnes adds that some elections are close enough to be decided by a few thousand votes. What's more, hundreds of thousands of college students are eligible to vote.

Now Melissa is embarrassed. The weakness of her view has been exposed in front of other students. She launches an attack on Agnes. "You have no business lecturing me about right and wrong. Just last week you cut Friday's classes so you could go home early, and then you lied to your instructors about being sick. Stop being a hypocrite, Agnes."

Even if this attack on Agnes is true, it has nothing to do with the issue of college students voting. It's merely a way for Melissa to save face.

In all these errors of reaction, ego gets in the way of critical thinking. It's in your long-term interest to acknowledge error and learn from it. Doing so promotes knowledge and wisdom.

How would Melissa respond if she practiced critical thinking? She would focus on Agnes's idea rather than on Agnes as a person. And since the idea seems reasonable, Melissa would probe it further before dismissing it. She could say, "Perhaps I'm mistaken. What steps are needed to vote by absentee ballot?" Then if Agnes's answer showed that the process is simple, Melissa could respond, "I guess you're right."

By acting this way, Melissa would not lose face. In fact, the other students could have been impressed at her flexibility and willingness to admit a mistake.

Straw man

As its name suggests, this error involves make-believe. Specifically, the error means pretending someone has said something that she has not said, and then denouncing her for saying it.

Imagine this situation: Someone has proposed that your school's attendance policy be revised to permit unlimited absences from class without penalty. You argue against the proposal, claiming that students who attend class sporadically slow the pace of learning for others and degrade the quality of class discussion.

Then someone responds to your argument as follows: "I take exception to your view. You say that adults should be treated as children, that students must leave their constitutional rights at the college gate, and that individuals whose work obligations sometimes force them to miss class are inferior creatures deserving of punishment."

Those stirring words, which bear no relation to reality, constitute the error of straw man. They attribute to you something you did not say. To avoid the error of straw man, listen to or read others' arguments carefully. Focus your criticism on what was actually said or clearly implied.

EXERCISE #38

Consider each of the four errors of reaction. Think of times when you committed them and describe these situations. Explain how you reacted and what consequences resulted. Then decide how you might have avoided the error and how the consequences might have been different. (If you can't think of an error of your own, identify one you encountered through reading or observation.)

Explaining away

_____
_____
_____
_____
_____
_____

Shifting the burden of proof

_____
_____
_____
_____
_____
_____

Attacking the person

_____
_____
_____
_____
_____
_____

Straw man

_____
_____
_____
_____
_____
_____

Errors can multiply

Errors would be costly enough if they occurred singly and separately. Yet in many cases one error invites another and that leads to several more. It's natural for us to want knowledge and wisdom. (Have you ever met anyone who *wanted* to be ignorant and foolish?) And with only a small investment of imagination, people can go from wanting it to pretending they have it and from there to seeing the world in a self-serving way.

The resulting errors of perception pave the way for errors of judgment. Examples are jumping to conclusions that flatter our viewpoint, assuming too much, or ignoring important distinctions. And once we embrace errors of judgment, express them to others, and hear them criticized, we are tempted to commit errors of reaction to save face.

Understanding the ways in which errors tend to multiply can help you think critically.

PRACTICING CRITICAL THINKING #12

Add your thoughtful reflection on the following observation in the space provided.

Observation

Many people reason that because everyone has a right to his or her opinion, everyone's opinion should be treated with respect and never challenged or disputed.

Reflection

_____

_____

_____

_____

_____

_____

_____

_____

_____

_____

_____

_____

_____

_____

_____

_____

_____

Practicing Critical Thinking #13

Look back at the list of observations you prepared in response to Practicing Critical Thinking #10 in Chapter Three. Select one of those observations, restate it below, and then add your reflections, as explained in Chapter One. Observations, remember, are interesting issues, statements that appear insightful (or mistaken), probing questions, ideas that may have wider implications, or anything else that you wish to understand more fully. Examples could include an incident, process, or procedure. Reflections are your thoughtful analysis of the observations.

Observation

_____
_____
_____
_____
_____
_____

Reflection

_____
_____
_____
_____
_____

Practicing Critical Thinking #14

Add your thoughtful reflection on the following observation in the space provided.

Observation

Psychologist Abraham Maslow explained the hierarchy of human needs by using the figure of a pyramid. *(see illustration below)* The lower needs, he believed, must be met before the higher needs are pursued. At the bottom of his pyramid are physiological needs (food, shelter, clothing). Then comes the need for belongingness and love. Above that comes self-esteem, then aesthetic and intellectual needs. At the top, representing the highest need, is self-actualization.

Austrian psychiatrist Viktor Frankl challenged this order. He argued that self-transcendence—forgetting about self and seeking challenging tasks to add meaning to one's existence—is the highest human need. He also believed that self-actualization cannot be pursued but comes only by achieving self-transcendence. Several decades have passed since these two views were first presented, and in the United States Maslow's has been more influential.

Reflection

_____
_____
_____
_____
_____
_____
_____
_____

PRACTICING CRITICAL THINKING #15

List below any observations you made since you completed your response to Practicing Critical Thinking #11 in Chapter Three. (Note: this Exercise will be repeated at the end of other chapters. Record any observations that you make between chapters in the following chapter.)

Interesting issues you would like to address when you have more time:

_____
_____
_____
_____
_____

Statements that appear to be unusually insightful. (They may have been made by authors, instructors, fellow students, or anyone else.)

_____
_____
_____

Statements that seem to be shallow or mistaken. Choose a statement serious enough that you want to know more about its flaws and perhaps respond to them.

_____
_____
_____
_____
_____
_____
_____

Questions that have arisen from your reading or listening or have otherwise occurred to you and seem worth pursuing.

_____
_____
_____
_____
_____
_____
_____

Ideals or situations that seem to have wider implications.

_____
_____
_____
_____
_____
_____

Anything you have experienced or heard about—for example, an incident, a process, or a procedure—that you wish to understand more fully.

_____
_____
_____
_____
_____

Name_____Date____/____/____

1 *When do errors of perception occur? How do they affect our thinking?*

2 *Define each of the following errors of perception and give one example of each.*
Use different examples from those in the text.

"Mine is better" thinking

Selective perception

Gullibility and skepticism

Bias toward the majority or minority

Pretending to know

Bias for or against change

Either/or thinking

3 *When do errors of judgment occur?*

4 *Define each of the following errors of judgment and give one example of each.
Use different examples from those in the text.*

Double standard

Irrelevant criterion

Overgeneralization or stereotyping

Hasty conclusion

Unwarranted assumption

Failure to make a distinction

Oversimplification

QUIZ
CONTINUED

5 *Explain what errors of reaction are and when they occur.*

6 *Define each of the following errors of reaction and give one example of each. Use different examples from those presented in the text.*

Explaining away

Shifting the burden of proof

Attacking the person

Straw man

5.
Applying Critical Thinking

IN THIS CHAPTER

Thinking critically about commercials.
Look for glittering generalities, empty comparisons, meaningless slogans, testimonials, and transfers.

Thinking critically about print advertising.
Advertisers choose every word and picture with an aim in mind—to sell a product, service, or idea. Analyze print advertisements.

Thinking critically about television programming.
Consider whether television viewing promotes habits that hinder critical thinking.

Thinking critically about music.
Critics say that popular music promotes antisocial attitudes; musicians deny the charge and decry censorship. Decide for yourself.

Thinking critically about magazines.
Consider whether popular magazines glorify the sensational or merely give the public what it wants.

Thinking critically about newspapers.
Hone your critical thinking skills on editorials and letters to the editor.

Expressing your ideas persuasively.
Complete the thinking process, focus on your viewpoint, choose a suitable organization, provide evidence, use an exact and lively style, vary paragraph length, and proofread.

THINKING CRITICALLY ABOUT
commercials

A DVERTISERS SPEND BILLIONS OF DOLLARS a year on commercials. The cost of just one fifteen-second commercial can exceed $500,000. In many cases, advertising goes beyond presenting the product or service. Advertisers stimulate viewers through appeals to desires: to be youthful, sexually appealing, successful, loved, or accepted by others. In advertising language, the aim is to "sell the sizzle, not the steak."

Former advertising executive Jerry Mander claims that advertising exists only to create needs for products. The trick, he says, is to make people feel discontented. And the standard advertising formula for doing so is to (1) gain the audience's attention, (2) arouse their interest, (3) stimulate a desire for the product, and (4) make the sales pitch.

The design of a commercial (or print ad), Mander explains, is no casual affair. Advertisers employ thousand of psychologists, behavioral scientists, perception researchers, and sociologists. These experts identify deep-seated human needs and desires, insecurities and fears. Then they determine how these can be used to the advertiser's advantage.

The techniques of advertising are the techniques of propaganda. Among the most common are the following:

Bandwagon
This technique creates the impression that everyone is buying the product or service. It appeals to the viewer's urge to conform.

Glittering generality
Here the advertiser uses words and phrases to imply excellence and uniqueness. Few specifics are offered. "Amazing new discovery," "now a stunning breakthrough," and "unheard-of softness" are examples of glittering generality.

Empty comparison

This technique uses words such as *better, bigger,* and *more* (as in "more economical") without completing the comparison. What, for example, does "greater cleaning power" mean? Greater than last year? Greater than the competition? Such a statement seems to make a serious claim. And yet we can't hold the advertiser responsible for it because we aren't sure just what is being claimed.

Meaningless slogan

Most large companies have slogans designed to create a positive impression. These create pleasant images but promise little.

United Airlines' slogan, "Fly the friendly skies," is designed to associate that airline with friendliness. "AT&T—The Right Choice" tries to link the act of choosing a telephone company with AT&T. This is a clever idea at a time when AT&T customers can choose a rival long-distance service. Another slogan is "Michelin . . . because so much is riding on your tires," and with these words we see pictures of adorable babies. The aim: viewers will associate buying Michelin tires with protecting their children.

Testimonial

A testimonial is an endorsement for a product or service. Actors, musicians, sports figures, and other well-known people are paid substantial sums of money to appear in commercials, lending their credibility and celebrity status to products. The words they speak may be written by someone else, and viewers often know this. Even so, advertisers still hope we'll associate the celebrity with the product or service.

Transfer

One common kind of transfer is the voice-over. Here the celebrity never appears in the commercial but acts as off-camera narrator. Even if the viewer cannot name the speaker, the voice may be familiar and make the message more appealing.

Another kind of transfer involves objects instead of people. For example, the Statue of Liberty or the flag could be shown with a product or service. Showing these symbols arouses strong positive feelings in many people. Advertisers want viewers to transfer those feelings to the product.

A less obvious use of transfer is the "party scene," where we see people enjoying themselves. The product, such as beer or a wine cooler, may be shown as creating the good time. Or the product may be a new car merely included in the scene.

The standard commercial break consists of four fifteen-second commercials. The average number of commercials included in an hour of television viewing is forty-four. If you watch four hours of television a day you encounter 176 appeals designed to short-circuit your critical thinking and create an artificial desire or need. Your best safeguard against this manipulation is to use your critical thinking skills.

EXERCISE #39

Watch at least two hours of television. Pay close attention to the commercials. For this assignment the programs themselves are unimportant. If you wish, do some other activity between commercial breaks.

As you observe each commercial, note the product or service advertised, the scenes shown, and the people on camera. Also listen for the narrator, music, and other sounds.

Next, select three of the commercials you observed. On a separate sheet of paper, describe each commercial and then analyze it by answering the following questions:

• *Does the commercial motivate the viewers to think or merely appeal to their emotions? Explain.*

• *What hopes, fears, or desires is the commercial designed to exploit? How?*

• *What attitudes and values does the commercial promote—for example, attitudes about success and happiness? How does the commercial promote them? Do you share these attitudes and values?*

• *Does the commercial use propaganda techniques? How?*

• *Would you classify this commercial as fair or unfair persuasion? What's the evidence for your view?*

EXERCISE #40

Calculate the average attention shifts occurring during commercials. Proceed as follows.

Watch any half-hour or hour program. When a commercial break occurs, keep your eyes focused on the television set. Each time a new image appears on the screen, make a tally on the page. (Use a separate sheet of paper for this tally.) When the next commercial appears, resume your tally on a new line.

At the end of the program, divide the number of lines into the grand total of stroke tallies. The answer will be the average attention shifts occurring during commercials for that program.

Summarize your findings in the space provided and then answer the following questions:

Number of tallies (images) _____
Number of lines (commercials) _____
Average attention shifts during the commercials _____

Were you surprised at the number of attention shifts you found per commercial? Explain

_____
_____
_____
_____
_____

What possible reasons might advertising agencies have for changing images at that rate? Which of those reasons seems most likely? Explain.

_____
_____
_____
_____
_____

Television commercials in the 1950s and 1960s were one minute long and contained relatively few images. Typically, one or more people talked about the product as they displayed it. In the 1970s and 1980s commercials were thirty seconds long and contained more images. Today's commercials are fifteen seconds in length and contain considerably more images. What effect, if any, could this change have had on academic performance? Job performance? Personal relationships? Explain your thoughts carefully.

_____
_____
_____
_____
_____
_____
_____
_____
_____
_____

EXERCISE #41

Based on your analysis in Exercises #39 and #40, do you think the Federal Communications Commission should change the standards for commercials? What restrictions, if any, should they impose? On a separate sheet of paper, write a composition of at least several paragraphs supporting your view. (You may wish to consult the guidelines in "Expressing your ideas persuasively" in Chapter Five.)

PRACTICING CRITICAL THINKING #16

If you watch television, you've probably encountered some or all of the commercial slogans shown below in the Observation column. Reflect on these slogans individually, or as a group, in light of this and previous chapters.

Observation	Reflection
"Just do it." (Nike slogan)	
"Image is everything." (Canon slogan)	
"Life is short—play hard." (Reebok slogan)	
"On planet Reebok there are no rules."	
"Why ask why? Try Bud dry." (Budweiser slogan)	
Voice asks, *"What should I drink?"* Narrator says, *"Give your brain a rest. Try some Sprite."*	
"Though we carry over 160,000 passengers a day, we serve each of them one at a time." (USAir slogan)	
"Red Wolf is here. Follow your instincts." (Red Wolf beer slogan)	
"We measure success one investor at a time." (Dean Witter slogan)	

THINKING CRITICALLY ABOUT
PRINT ADVERTISING

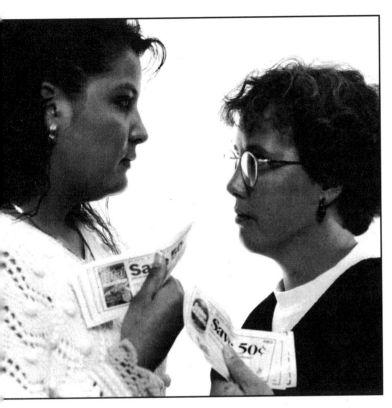

Advertisers know how to make a print ad effective. Every detail must contribute to the overall message. They take great care in choosing and arranging every word and picture. Analyzing print ads involves studying these choices.

Critics charge that print ads often deceive people. For example, cigarette advertising presents smoking as glamorous, picturing smokers as attractive people laughing in festive gatherings.

Certain other ads, the critics argue, are offensive. One ad for Masquerade perfume pictures a man and a woman in a highly aroused sexual state. The caption reads, "Unleash your fantasies." A Guess jeans ad shows a woman being backed into a fence by cowboys. Obsession perfume ads show us a beautiful but frightened woman and several people who are clinging to her. The slogan that accompanies this picture: "No one could protect her from the passion she inspired."

Some viewers think these ads aggravate the problem of violence against women. They feel the ads carry a message: women want to be assaulted.

Another charge is that advertising can harm children. Bombardment by propaganda makes children gullible, says this argument, and children are less able to resist manipulation.

Defenders of advertising deny all this. They argue that advertising is simply honest persuasion. The appeals in ads, they say, are the same appeals parents use to instill values in their children.

L IKE TELEVISION COMMERCIALS, print advertising is designed to sell a product, service, or idea. Such advertising may appeal to the desire for happiness or the need for belonging, acceptance, and love. However, the techniques print ads use are more limited. They cannot use sound or show motion. They're strictly visual and static.

EXERCISE #42

Visit the magazine section of your campus library. Skim at least a half-dozen magazines, looking for interesting print ads. Don't limit yourself to magazines you already know. The wider your assortment, the more varied the ads you'll find. Next, select three ads and describe each one. Then analyze them by answering the questions below. If you wish, attach a photocopy of the ads.

• Does the advertisement motivate the viewers to think or merely appeal to their emotions? Explain.

• What hopes, fears, or desires, if any, is the ad designed to exploit? How does it appeal to them?

• What attitudes or values, if any, does the ad promote—for example, attitudes about success and happiness?

• How does it promote them? Do you share those attitudes and values?

• What propaganda techniques, if any, are used? Explain how they are used.

• Would you classify this ad as fair or unfair persuasion? What's the evidence for your view?

First ad
Description:

_____

_____

_____

_____

_____

Analysis:

_____

_____

_____

_____

_____

_____

Second ad
Description:

_____

_____

_____

_____

_____

_____

Analysis:

_____

_____

_____

_____

_____

_____

Third ad
Description:

_____

_____

_____

_____

_____

Analysis:

_____

_____

_____

_____

_____

THINKING CRITICALLY ABOUT
TELEVISION programming

B Y HIGH SCHOOL GRADUATION, the average person has spent 11,000 hours in the classroom and 22,000 hours watching television. All things being equal, television has twice as much impact on a person's mind as formal education.

Yet not all things are equal. Television producers have more means to maintain audience attention. They can use music to manipulate emotions. Directors can shift scenes to sustain interest and use applause tracks to cue responses. All this is evidence for television's impact. The question continues to be debated: is that impact mainly positive or negative?

In 1961 Newton Minow, then chairman of the Federal Communications Commission, called television a "vast wasteland." Twenty-five years later his judgment was essentially the same. In Minow's view and those of other critics, television seriously underestimates the viewer's intelligence.

Other critics of television programming argue that it also creates mental habits and attitudes that hinder learning. These critics advance the following arguments:

- By keeping young people away from books, television denies them opportunities to develop imagination.
- Television aims programming at the lowest common denominator. This deprives young people of intellectual challenge.
- By feeding young people a steady diet of slang and clichés, television hinders their language skills.
- Television limits game show questions to who? what? where? and when? They seldom ask how? and never why? This creates the impression that knowledge of trivia is the only knowledge worth having. It also implies that careful analysis of issues is unnecessary or boring.
- Television uses the narrative approach for most of its programming. Examples are soap operas, situation comedies, movies, and dramatic series. By doing so, television denies young people exposure to critical thinking. (Such thinking is more commonly expressed in analysis than in narrative.)

• Television fills the roster of talk shows with celebrities rather than authorities. By doing so, television creates the impression that it's not what you know but how well known you are that's important.

Jerry Mander has analyzed why television has failed to live up to expectations. In *Four Arguments for the Elimination of Television*, he claims that television has a number of inherent limitations that cannot easily be overcome. For one thing, it is an artificial environment that viewers have no hand in creating. Even on newscasts, we see only what others decide to show us, and always from their particular perspective and according to their priorities. For every news item included in the news, thousands are excluded.

Another limitation is that less visible things don't play as well on television as more visible ones. That is why we see more angry expressions than happy ones, more fistfights and shootings than calm discussions, more car chases and explosions than tranquil scenes, more passionate sexual encounters than gentler expressions of friendship, caring, and tenderness.

A third limitation, according to Mander, is that the everyday pace of reality is not well suited to television. To make their stories interesting, programmers have to compress events. TV heroes are confronted by one dangerous situation after another, whereas in real life many tedious hours of inactivity intervene. Regular television viewing can create the unrealistic expectation that real life ought to be one peak experience after another.

The expectation is reinforced by the news. Reporters prefer to cover sensational stories. When they are forced to cover an ordinary event they often seek out the most dramatic or sensational aspect—for example, the single angry outburst in an otherwise calm and productive city council meeting. Antisocial behavior is deemed more newsworthy than social behavior.

The inherent limitations of television result in a number of biases in selecting program material. Mander finds more than thirty, including the following:

A bias for war over peace, and violence over nonviolence.
A bias for superficiality over depth, simplification over balance.
A bias for feelings of conflict over feelings of agreement.
A bias for lust over satisfaction, anger over tranquility, jealousy over acceptance.
A bias for competition over cooperation.
A bias for materialism over spirituality.
A bias for the bizarre over the usual, the fixed over the evolutionary, the static over the dynamic.

If these charges of Manders and others are valid, television may be responsible for a number of social problems. For example, it may cause or aggravate many of the difficulties students experience in school, some of which cause them to drop out before graduation. Television may also be responsible for the tendency of many people to settle for mediocrity rather than strive for excellence.

The following Exercises direct your critical thinking to these questions: Is television programming harming our country and its citizens? If so, what can be done to correct that condition? If not, what can be done to make television programming an even more positive influence?

EXERCISE #43

Select a television game show and watch it for one or more programs. Note the way the game is played, the kinds of questions asked, and the time allowed for responses. Also note background effects such as music, lights, or revolving wheels and any other significant details about the show. Then analyze what you've seen. Answer these and any other relevant questions:

• *How intellectually demanding is the show?*

_____

_____

_____

• *What is the show's appeal to viewers?*

_____

_____

_____

• *What habits or attitudes could this show develop or reinforce in regular adult viewers? In children? Will these habits and attitudes help or hinder life in school, on the job, and at home?*

_____

_____

_____

   Next, on a separate sheet of paper, write a composition of at least several paragraphs. Explain and support your reactions.

EXERCISE #44

Select a television situation comedy and watch it for one or more programs. Then analyze what you saw. Answer these and other relevant questions:

• *How original was the story line? Can you remember any other show you've seen with a similar plot?*

_____

_____

_____

_____

• *What attitudes and values did the show encourage? Do you share them?*

_____

_____

_____

• *Did the characters rise above stereotypes: the dumb blonde, the know-it-all teenagers, and so on?*

_____

_____

_____

• *Would you have laughed if the show had had no laugh track? How original were the jokes?*

_____

_____

_____

   Next, on a separate sheet of paper, write a composition of at least several paragraphs. Explain and support your reactions.

EXERCISE #45

Choose a television drama—a soap opera, detective or western show, or a movie. To help yourself think critically, pick a show you don't normally see. Watch the show and then analyze what you saw. Answer these and any other relevant questions:

• Which characters did the show present favorably? What was the main action taken by each of those characters during the show?

_____

_____

_____

_____

_____

• Think about the characters you chose in the above question. What view would each express on the following topics?

Reasoning with others:

_____

_____

Violence:

_____

_____

Sexual relationships:

_____

_____

Marriage:

_____

_____

Authority:

_____

_____

Success:

_____

_____

• Did the show include any incidents of violence and/or destruction? If so, describe them and explain whether their depiction was essential to the plot.
• Were people or principles betrayed during the show? If so, describe each incident and explain whether the betrayal was presented in a positive or negative light.

_____

_____

_____

_____

_____

_____

_____

• Did the show emphasize antagonism or harmony? Were issues resolved peacefully or violently? Explain.

_____

_____

_____

_____

Write a composition of at least several paragraphs, based on your analysis, on a separate sheet of paper. Explain whether the show you watched promoted desirable attitudes and habits.

EXERCISE #46

Skim the television talk show listings. Then select a show and watch it. Analyze what you saw, answering these and any other relevant questions:

• *What was the show's theme or discussion topic?*

_____

_____

_____

• *What fields did the guests represent: show business, education, particular professions, or others? Are the guests associated with specific attitudes, values, behaviors? If so, describe those attitudes, values, or behaviors.*

_____

_____

_____

_____

• *What was the reason why each appeared on the show? For example, an author may have published a new book or an actress starred in a just-released film.*

_____

_____

_____

• *What kinds of questions did the host ask? Professional questions? Personal questions?*

_____

_____

_____

• *Were any specific attitudes and values encouraged? If so, what were they? Do you share them?*

_____

_____

_____

• *How much time did the host allow for each answer? Did the guest have an opportunity to elaborate on answers? How much time was devoted to each guest?*

_____

_____

_____

• *How many times was the discussion interrupted by commercial breaks?*

_____

_____

_____

Next, write a composition of at least several paragraphs on a separate sheet of paper. Focus on this question: would regular viewing of talk shows like the one you watched be good preparation for the probing discussions conducted in college classrooms?

EXERCISE #47

Watch the evening newscast of the three major networks. Compare their presentation of the news. Answer these and any other relevant questions:

• *How much time, on the average, was given to each news story?*

_____

_____

_____

• *What details did the newscasters focus on? What questions did they pass over? Did you want answers to any of these questions?*

_____

_____

_____

• How were the newscasts similar? Look, for example, at the number and gender of the newscasters, construction of the studio sets, and each show's format. How were the shows different?

_____

_____

_____

_____

• How many commercial breaks appeared during the newscast?

_____

_____

_____

_____

• Do you think the news stories gave a fair picture of world events?

_____

_____

_____

_____

• What other types of stories might have been included?

_____

_____

_____

_____

Decide how the news broadcasts you watched could help or hinder intellectual development. On a separate sheet of paper, write a composition of at least several paragraphs explaining and supporting your views.

EXERCISE #48

Consider the observations and judgments of the various kinds of television programming from the previous Exercises. Decide what changes would improve television programming. Then write a letter to the Federal Communications Commission. State your ideas for improving programming and give reasons for acting on those ideas.

_____

_____

_____

_____

_____

_____

_____

_____

_____

_____

_____

_____

_____

_____

_____

_____

_____

_____

_____

_____

_____

_____

_____

THINKING CRITICALLY ABOUT *music*

RIDICULING ANOTHER GENERATION'S music has long been a popular pastime. Someone once defined an opera as a place where anything that is too dumb to be spoken is sung. Another person observed that classical music threatens to develop a tune with every other bar and then disappoints us. A third termed jazz an appeal to the emotions by an attack on the nerves. Another, writing of rock music, suggested that the proper pitch for most electrical guitars is right out the window, followed by the player.

Yet the fact that each generation prefers its own music does not mean that all criticism is without merit. It is important to keep this in mind in evaluating contemporary music.

Music has changed greatly in the past half-century, perhaps more so than in any comparable period in history. In the late 1940s two older musical traditions continued in vogue. One was Big Band music, played for ballroom dancing ranging from the elegant foxtrot to frenetic jitterbugging. The other was jazz.

The 1950s brought rock and roll with its very different beat, both literally and figuratively. It may have lacked the refinement and style of jazz, but there was no doubting its raucous energy. From the days of Elvis Presley's "Blue Suede Shoes" to the present, rock and roll has undergone several transformations, notably to acid rock and then heavy metal. And other music forms have become popular—reggae, for example, and rap.

The differences between 1940s music and today's music go beyond the overall sound or the beat. Because no amplification existed then, the loudest jazz band was much quieter than today's groups. In those days, too, singers still "crooned" ballads in the manner of Bing Crosby and Frank Sinatra. Lyrics were meant to be understood and the singer's voice was regarded as another fine instrument to be used with precision to produce pleasant, melodious sounds. Singers wore hair styles no different from those of business people. All that has changed.

A more significant difference than these is the ideas and attitudes conveyed by the lyrics themselves and the mannerisms that accompany them. Today's lyrics and stage antics would have been unimaginable fifty years ago. Many popular videos celebrate the destruction of property, rape, child abuse, incest, sadism, murder, and suicide. On-screen images depict these behaviors in graphic detail. And the average age of the audience that watches them is between 14 and 16.

Critics of contemporary music have charged that it is undermining the fundamental values of society and causing antisocial attitudes and behavior, including crime. Spokespeople for the music industry tend to dismiss such criticism, claiming that musicians are only exercising their right of free expression and no one can be harmed by that. The Exercises that follow will give you an opportunity to examine this issue.

EXERCISE #49

Visit a music store and examine a number of current CD's, cassettes, or albums. Note the cover design, song titles, and lyrics. Listen to releases from major groups. Then, on a separate sheet of paper, list each CD, cassette, or album you examined and record your observations.

EXERCISE #50

Analyze your findings about the music you researched. Answer these and any other relevant questions:

• On the basis of your inquiry, would you say the music conveys positive values and attitudes?

_____

_____

_____

_____

_____

_____

_____

• Suppose that people applied the messages in the song lyrics to their lives. In what specific ways would their behavior be affected? Would the consequences be desirable or undesirable?

_____

_____

_____

_____

_____

_____

_____

_____

• Are the complaints against popular music justified? If not, why not? If so, what action do you recommend? Who should take that action? Government? The music industry?

_____

_____

_____

_____

_____

_____

Now, present your view in a composition of at least several paragraphs. Include appropriate explanation and support.

_____

_____

_____

_____

_____

_____

_____

_____

THINKING CRITICALLY ABOUT
MAGAZINES

Literally hundreds of magazines are available on a variety of subjects, including animals, art, investment, computers, entertainment, hobbies, home and garden, nature, religion, science, and travel. Among the most widely read are news magazines such as *Time, Newsweek,* and *U.S. News and World Report.* Also popular are the general interest tabloid magazines such as *People, The Star,* and *The National Enquirer.*

Some magazines publish only staff-written articles. Others solicit articles from freelance writers. Every magazine has its own specific areas of interest, format, editorial requirements, and point of view.

A magazine's target audience may be broad, as in the case of most news magazines, or narrow. There are magazines for political conservatives

and magazines for liberals, some for men and others for women. Age, marital status, and work status are further areas of specialization. *McCall's,* for example, is published for women in general; *Redbook,* for young mothers, age 25–44; *Cosmopolitan,* for working women, 18–35, single, married, or divorced.

Among the most common criticisms of news and/or general interest magazines are the following:

- That the editorial biases of news magazines often result in a lack of objectivity in reporting, particularly on issues related to the bias. A secular bias, for example, might prejudice the treatment of religion; a liberal political bias might prejudice the treatment of conservative proposals or programs.
- That general interest magazines promote shallowness and superficiality by focusing on the details of celebrities' lives, particularly scandalous details.
- Than many magazines allow their choice and treatment of subject matter to be influenced, and often compromised, by their advertisers.
- That many magazines tend to reinforce the values of popular culture—in particular, impulsiveness, self-indulgence, and instant gratification—rather than the values of traditional culture.

The following Exercises invite you to apply critical thinking and decide whether these charges are valid. To complete these assignments, you may decide to visit a newsstand, library, or bookstore.

EXERCISE #51

Examine the current editions of Time, Newsweek, and U.S. News and World Report. *Read the cover story of each magazine. That story may be the same in all three magazines or different in each. Compare the treatment the subject or subjects receive. For each subject, decide which magazine's treatment is most biased and which is least biased. Support your findings.*

Your decision and support:

_____

_____

_____

_____

_____

EXERCISE #53

Examine an edition of each of the following publications: The Star, The National Enquirer, and People. *Read the articles, the special sections, and the advice columns. Also sample the ads and look closely at the photographs. Then answer these questions:*

• Suppose that a stranger to this country were to draw a conclusion about our society's attitudes and values just from reading these publications. What conclusion do you think she would draw? What about these periodicals makes you think so?

_____

_____

_____

_____

_____

_____

• Do you think these publications merely reflect our society's attitudes and values? Or do they also help shape those attitudes and values? Explain.

_____

_____

_____

_____

_____

_____

EXERCISE #52

Check the covers of the current issues of the following magazines: Cosmopolitan, McCall's, Esquire, Redbook, and Psychology Today. *Make a list of the articles featured on the covers. Do the similarities or differences in the topics raise any questions in your mind? Do they suggest any conclusions? If so, explain.*

_____

_____

_____

_____

_____

_____

_____

_____

_____

• What changes in format and emphasis would you recommend to improve these publications? On a separate sheet of paper, present your response in a composition of several paragraphs.

THINKING CRITICALLY ABOUT
newspapers

T HE NEWSPAPER IS an ancient form of communication that can be traced back to about 59 B.C. when the Roman *Acta Diurna* was posted in public places. Its greatest development, however, occurred after the invention of printing in the fifteenth century. More recently, the invention of the telegraph, the photocomposition process, and the communications satellite have made news gathering and publication faster and more efficient.

Other inventions, however, have challenged the newspaper's position as the leading provider of information. The most notable of these inventions have been radio and television, and the personal computer has similar potential. All three make news available at the flip of a switch,

whereas the newspaper is available, in most cases, only once a day and must be delivered.

The newspaper has a further disadvantage—it requires the effort of reading. In contrast, broadcast news is obtained effortlessly, and in a conveniently rapid pace, in moving pictures. In reaction to this handicap, the newspaper industry has simplified and shortened stories. The most extreme example of this approach is the *USA Today* format.

Another change in print journalism over the last few decades concerns the treatment of fact and opinion. Traditionally, news stories presented only facts, objectively and without comment. A special place was reserved for commentary—the op-ed page. (The term is short for opinion-editorial.) There the reader would find editorials presenting the newspaper's official point of view on issues of the day, letters expressing readers' reactions to previous news stories, and opinion essays written by professional columnists.

Today's newspapers have an op-ed page, with editorials, letters, and columns. But opinion is no longer carefully screened out of news stories. Many journalists, in fact, blend their interpretations and personal judgments into the news. Only the alert reader will understand where reporting ends and editorializing begins.

The op-ed page continues to be the most rewarding part of the newspaper because it is filled with lively analysis of current issues. The following exercises invite you to apply critical thinking skills to that page.

EXERCISE #54

Choose the largest newspaper in your area or a newspaper serving a larger audience, such as USA Today. *Read the main editorial of the day. Also read any news story mentioned in the editorial. Then, on a separate sheet of paper, answer the following questions:*

• What position does the editor take on the issue? What support does he or she offer for this position?

• What other positions could be taken on the issue? How might those positions be supported? Before answering these questions, you may wish to research the issue by visiting the library or interviewing experts.

• What are the strengths and weaknesses?

• What position is most reasonable in light of the evidence? Present your response in a composition of at least several paragraphs. Another option is to write your response as a letter to the editor. If you do this, consider sending the letter to the newspaper.

PRACTICING CRITICAL THINKING #17

Reflect on the following observation on a separate sheet of paper. Decide if the observation is significant, and if so, in what way.

Observation

In a District of Columbia study some years ago, a group of children ages 7 to 12 were asked to name as many presidents and brands of alcoholic beverages as they could. On average, they named 4.8 presidents, and 5.2 beverages. (Edward Klein, "The Best and Worst of Everything," *Parade*, 30 December 1990, 5)

EXERCISE #55

Select an opinion column or a letter to the editor that interests you. Examine it critically. If appropriate, research the issue further. Then, on a separate piece of paper, write a composition of at least several paragraphs stating and supporting your position on the issue. You may agree with the article or letter in the newspaper, disagree with it, or agree in part. Attach either a summary or copy of the original article or letter.

PRACTICING CRITICAL THINKING #18

On a separate sheet of paper, select an observation you have made since beginning this chapter and reflect on it as you have previous observations. (If you prefer, select an observation you recorded in a previous chapter but never analyzed.)

EXPRESSING YOUR IDEAS
Persuasively

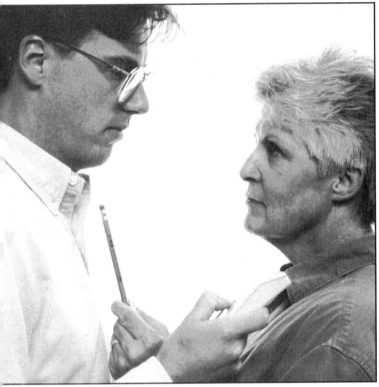

PREVIOUS CHAPTERS have presented strategies for critical thinking. You have completed many exercises and activities and increased your skill in evaluating ideas and arguments. In the process you have undoubtedly become more aware that other people are as committed to their views as you are to yours. Changing minds is not an easy task. This final article addresses the important subject of how to communicate your ideas persuasively.

The audience for persuasive writing is typically mixed: some readers will agree thoroughly with your view; others will partly agree and partly disagree; still others will disagree entirely. Writing for people who agree is no challenge. Writing for those who partly agree is difficult because you have no sure way of knowing exactly where their disagreement lies. For this reason, it is best to write for those who disagree entirely. They will always be the most critical readers.

Aim to demonstrate that your view is more reasonable than competing views. Try to anticipate the questions and challenges critical readers are likely to raise about your viewpoint. Answer those questions and address those challenges clearly and thoroughly.

The following guidelines will help you get started. For more detailed information about persuasive writing, ask your campus librarian or bookstore manger to recommend a good composition handbook.

Guideline 1: Complete the thinking process first

Some people begin their persuasive writing hoping to develop their thoughts about the issue as they are writing. The result is usually a confused, disorganized, unpersuasive composition.

You can avoid this fate. Before presenting your ideas to others, finish your analysis. Know what you think about the issue and the evidence for your view. (You may use writing as a tool of analysis to help yourself discover ideas.)

Guideline 2: Use your viewpoint as your controlling idea

The controlling idea in persuasive writing is the view you've decided is most reasonable. Chapter 1 discussed the thinking of one student, Jennifer, about astrology. After applying critical thinking, she decided that despite the fact that many well-known, educated people believe in astrology, it is a poor guide to everyday living.

If Jennifer were writing a persuasive composition on astrology, that would be her controlling idea. Everything else in the composition would serve to support that idea and present it convincingly.

Guideline 3: Choose a suitable organization

A simple, effective way to organize a persuasive composition is to present your information in the following order:

1. Your controlling idea.
2. Your first argument for this idea, with supporting evidence.
3. Your second argument and supporting evidence.
4. Your third argument (if you have one) and supporting evidence.

Writers often put their most powerful argument last. That way the readers' final impression is the strongest.

If you choose to use a formal introduction, place it before the controlling idea. Likewise, if you'd like a formal conclusion to sum up and reinforce your message, place it after your last argument.

Guideline 4: Support your view with evidence

In persuasive writing, what you think is important. Yet the evidence supporting your view is even more important. Getting others to change their views will take more than your say-so. Careful thinkers want good reasons for changing their minds.

You may recall that Jennifer supported her judgment on astrology with these reasons:

1. It is based on such superstitious beliefs as the association of the red planet, Mars, with blood and aggression.
2. It considers birth, rather than conception, as the time of greatest influence.
3. Its central tenet of planetary influence has not been modified as new planets have been discovered.

If Jennifer were writing a persuasive paper, she would present these reasons in more detail. She might also anticipate questions such as these: Is astrology based on other superstitions? What exactly do astrologers say about planetary influence at birth versus conception? Why did the discovery of new planets require that the planetary influence idea be modified?

Jennifer could answer these questions and consider other approaches. For example, she could discuss research studies, introduce examples of specific horoscope advice from magazines and newspapers, explain astrology's history, and quote or paraphrase authorities on the subject of astrology.

You may find one or more of these approaches useful in your persuasive writing.

Guideline 5: Be exact, yet lively

Style is less important than substance. Even so, style can build or destroy the readers' confidence in you. Some fundamental rules of style are as follows:

Choose words that convey your idea exactly. Avoid using long words or fancy words just to impress your readers.

Cut unnecessary words. When you can, reduce a sentence to a clause, a clause to a phrase, a phrase to a word.

Vary your sentences. Occasionally combine several short sentences into a longer one. Begin sentences in different ways by changing the order of phrases and clauses.

Guideline 6: Vary your paragraph length

Effective paragraphs make writing easier to read and comprehend. Vary your paragraph length from five to fifteen lines. Ten lines is a good rough average. To keep the flow of your ideas clear, break paragraphs between two ideas rather than in the middle of an idea.

Guideline 7: Proofread your composition for acceptable punctuation, grammar, and usage

Professional writers make as many errors as amateurs. The difference is that professionals proofread and correct their work before others see it. Their example is worth imitating.

QUIZ

1 *Define each of the following terms:*

Bandwagon—

Glittering generality—

Empty comparison—

Meaningless slogan—

Testimonial—

Transfer—

2 *List some appeals often used in advertising. Give an actual example of each.*

3 *Describe criticisms commonly made of print advertising.*

4 *Newton Minow believes that television has improved significantly over the past quarter-century. True or false? Explain your answer.*

5 *Identify common criticisms of television programming.*

6 *Identify some criticisms commonly made of popular music.*

7 *Identify common criticisms of magazine publishing.*

EPILOGUE
Make the end a beginning

YOU'VE FINISHED reading this book and completed its Exercises and other opportunities to practice critical thinking. Now you have a choice. You can decide that this moment will mark the end of one more academic experience. If this is your choice, just consign the book to a box in your basement and let it gather dust. As memory fades, the experiences you had with this book will be lost.

There is an alternative. You can decide to make this book and critical thinking skills a vital part of your life. You can choose to make the end a beginning. One strategy is to buy a notebook and continue the journal you began here. As explained in Chapter One, a bound notebook no smaller than 6x9 inches is preferable. Use the left pages for recording observations; reserve the right pages for reflections on those observations. Since reflections are usually lengthier than observations, leave appropriate space between observations.

Here is a collection of quotations to help you get started. Some apply in many situations; others, in a limited number. A few may need qualification. All will provide excellent food for thought. *Bon appetit!*

If I am not for myself, who will be? If I am only for myself, what am I? —Rabbi Hillel

The cruelest lies are often told in silence. —Robert Louis Stevenson

Someone's boring me . . . I think it's me. —Dylan Thomas

Many people have played themselves to death. Many people have eaten and drunk themselves to death. Nobody ever thought himself to death. —Gilbert Highet

It is impossible to defeat an ignorant man in an argument. —William G. McAdoo

Each morning puts a man on trial and each evening passes judgment. —Roy L. Smith

A man has to live with himself, so he should see to it that he is always in good company. —Mencius

How glorious it is—and how painful—to be an exception. —Alfred de Musset

There was never an angry man that thought his anger unjust. —St. Francis de Sales

The man who most vividly realizes a difficulty is the man most likely to overcome it. —Joseph Farrell

You can tell the ideals of a nation by its advertisements. —Norman Douglas

To escape criticism—do nothing, say nothing, be nothing. —Elbert G. Hubbard

The true teacher defends his pupils against his own personal influence. —Bronson Alcott

That man is the richest whose pleasures are the cheapest. —Henry David Thoreau

To read without reflecting is like eating without digesting. —Edmund Burke

Bibliography

THE FOLLOWING BOOKS on critical thinking and related subjects can help you deepen your understanding and expand your skill.

Adams, James. *Conceptual Blockbusting.* W. W. Norton, New York, 1979.

Adler, Mortimer.
How to Read a Book. Simon and Schuster, New York, 1972.
Intellect: Mind Over Matter. Macmillan Publishing Co., New York, 1990.

Barker, Evelyn M. *Everyday Reasoning.* Prentice-Hall, Englewood Cliffs, New Jersey, 1981.

Barry, Vincent E., and Joel Rudinow. *Invitation to Critical Thinking.* Holt, Rinehart & Winston, New York, 1990.

Browne, Neil, and Stuart Keely. *Asking the Right Questions: A Guide to Critical Thinking.* Prentice-Hall, Englewood Cliffs, New Jersey, 1986.

Cederblom, J. B., and Paulsen, David W. *Critical Reasoning.* Wadsworth Publishing Co., Belmont, CA, 1986.

Chaffee, John. *Thinking Critically.* Houghton-Mifflin, New York, 1985.

Damer, Edward. *Attacking Faulty Reasoning.* Wadsworth Publishing Co., Belmont, CA, 1987.

DeBono, Edward. *Lateral Thinking.* Harper & Row, New York, 1970.

Engel, S. Morris. *With Good Reason: An Introduction to Informal Fallacies.* Third Edition. St. Martin's Press, New York, 1986.

Fisher, Alec. *The Logic of Real Arguments.* Cambridge University Press, New York, 1988.

Govier, Trudy. *A Practical Study of Argument.* Wadsworth Publishing Co., Belmont, CA, 1988.

Halpern, Diane. *Thought and Knowledge.* Lawrence Erlbaum, Hillsdale, NJ, 1984.

Hitchcock, David. *Critical Thinking: A Guide to Evaluating Information.* Methuen Publications, Toronto, Canada, 1983.

Hoaglund, John. *Critical Thinking.* Vale Press, Newport News, VA, 1984.

Johnson, Ralph, and J.A. Blair. *Logical Self-Defense.* McGraw-Hill, New York, 1983.

Kytle, Ray. *Clear Thinking for Composition.* McGraw-Hill Book Co., New York, 1987.

Lazere, Donald. *American Media and Mass Culture,* University of California Press, Berkeley, CA, 1987.

Mander, Jerry. *Four Arguments for the Elimination of Television,* Quill Publishing, New York, 1978.

Mayfield, Marlys. *Thinking for Yourself: Developing Critical Thinking Skills Through Writing.* Wadsworth Publishing Co., Belmont, CA, 1987.

Michalos, Alex C. *Improving Your Reasoning.* Prentice-Hall, Englewood Cliffs, New Jersey, 1986.

Miller, Robert K. *Informed Argument.* Harcourt Brace Jovanovich, San Diego, CA, 1989.

Missimer, Connie. *Good Arguments.* Prentice-Hall, Englewood Cliffs, NJ, 1986.

Moore, Brooke N. *Critical Thinking: Evaluating Claims and Arguments in Everyday Life.* Mayfield Publishing Co., Palo Alto, CA, 1989.

Moore, Edgar. *Creative and Critical Reasoning.* Houghton Mifflin Co., Boston, MA, 1984.

Nickerson, Raymond S. *Reflections on Reasoning.* L. Erlbaum, Hillsdale, New Jersey, 1986.

Nosich, Gerald. *Reasons and Arguments.* Wadsworth Publishing Co., Belmont, CA, 1982.

Paul, Richard. *Critical Thinking: What Every Person Needs to Survive in a Rapidly Changing World.* Center for Critical Thinking and Moral Critique, Sonoma State University, Rohnert Park, CA, 1990.

Perkins, David. *Knowledge as Design.* Lawrence Erlbaum, Hillsdale, NJ, 1986.

Postman, Neil. *Amusing Ourselves to Death.* Oxford University Press, New York, 1985.

Rosenthal, Peggy. *Words and Values.* Oxford University Press, New York, 1984.

Ruggiero, Vincent Ryan.
Thinking Critically About Ethical Issues. Mayfield Publishing Co., Mountain View, CA, 1992.

Beyond Feelings: A Guide to Critical Thinking, Mayfield Publishing Co., Mountain View, CA, 1995.

The Art of Thinking. Fourth Edition. Harper Collins, New York, 1995.

Warning: Nonsense Is Destroying America. Thomas Nelson, Nashville, TN, 1994.

Scriven, Michael. *Reasoning.* McGraw-Hill, New York, 1976.

Seech, Zachary. *Logic in Everyday Life: Practical Reasoning Skills.* Wadsworth Publishing Co., Belmont, CA, 1988

Shor, Ira. *Critical Thinking and Everyday Life,* University of Chicago Press, Chicago, IL, 1987

Siegel, Harvey. *Relativism Refuted.* Kluwer-Academic Publishers, Norwell, MA, 1987.

Toulmin, Stephen. *The Uses of Argument.* Cambridge University Press, New York, 1958.

Toulmin, Stephen E., Richard Rieke, and Alan Janik. *An Introduction to Reasoning.* Macmillan Publishing Co., New York, 1979.

Von Oech, Roger. *A Kick in the Seat of the Pants.* Harper & Row, New York, 1986.

Weddle, Perry. *Argument.* McGraw-Hill, New York, 1978.

Index

Abstract publications, 69
Active listening, 23
Advertising
    print, 106
    techniques of, 102–103
Alcott, Bronson, 125
Almanacs, 69
"And" relationships, 62
Arguments
    explanation of, 60
    finding competing views to,
    68–70
    sorting out disagreements
    to, 70–71
    testing for reasonableness of,
    72–74
    thinking of counter-, 26, 68
    types of, 9
    understanding, 62–63
Assumptions, 88–89
Attitudes, 48
    evaluation of your, 37
    explanation of, 36
    formation of, 35
    influences on, 36–37
Authorities, need to consult,
68

Bacon, Francis, 23
Bandwagon, 102
Bias
    for or against change, 85
    in television programming
    material, 109
    toward majority or
    minority, 84
Books, 22
Burke, Edmund, 125
Business Periodicals Index, 69
"But" relationships, 62

Clark, Marcia, 46
Commercials, 102–103
Common knowledge, 11
Comparison, 103

Competing views, 68–70
Complexity, 48–49
Computer data bases, 69
Concentration, 22
Confusion, 46
Contradiction, 9
Convictions, 20
Creative thinking, 3–4
Critical thinkers,
    characteristics of, 45–49
Critical thinking
    about commercials,
    102–103
    about magazines, 116
    about music, 114–115
    about newspapers, 118
    about print advertising, 106
    about television
    programming, 108–109
    contradiction as aid to, 9
    explanation of, 4, 24
    familiarity as obstacle to, 19
    function of convictions in,
    20
    importance of, 6
    instruction in, 5
    strategies for, 22–26
Curtsinger, Bill, 11

Data bases, 69
Daydreaming, 3
de Musset, Alfred, 125
de Sales, St. Francis, 125
Disagreements, 70–71
Distinctions, 89
Distractions, 22
Double standards, 87
Douglas, Norman, 125

Editorials
    keeping up with events
    through, 22
    in news magazines, 116
    in newspapers, 118
Editorials on File, 69"

Either/or" thinking, 85
Ellis, Albert, 5
Empty comparison, 103
Encyclopedia Americana, 69
Encyclopedias, 69
Epictetus, 14
Errors
    of judgment, 87–89
    multiplication of, 95
    of perception, 83–85
    of reaction, 92–94
Erskine, John, 14
Evidence
    evaluation of, 18–20, 48, 71
    explanation of, 18
    identification of, 62–63
    to support views, 121
    testing of, 72
Explaining away, 92
Eyewitness testimony, 10
Facts
    newspapers' treatment of,
    118
    separation of opinions from,
    10–11
Facts on File, 69
Familiarity, as obstacle to
    critical thinking, 19
Farrell, Joseph, 125

Generality, 102
Generalizations, 88
Gide, André 14, 82
Government publications, 69

Hasty conclusions, 88
Highet, Gilbert, 125
Hillel, Rabbi, 125
Honesty, 45–46
Hubbard, Elbert G., 125
Humanities Index, 69

Ideas
  contradiction of, 9
  evaluation of, 4
  formation of, 35
  persuasive expression of, 120–122
  production of, 3–4, 47
  reading for main, 62
  reasonableness of, 6
Illogical thinking, 5
Imagination, 26
Individuality
  development of, 34–35
  explanation of, 34
Information, 26
Intellectual independence, 49
Interviews, 68
Irrelevant criteria, 88

Judgment errors, 87–89

Knowledge
  common, 11
  connections between, 49
  listening to gain, 23
  pretending to have, 84–85
  refer to sources of, 26
  roots of, 22
Korzybski, Alfred, 84

Libraries, 68–69
Library catalogs, 69
Library staff, 69
Listening, 23

Magazines
  keeping up with events through, 22
  thinking critically about, 116
Mander, Jerry, 102, 109
Manipulation, 46
McAdoo, William G., 125
Mental habits, 40
Minow, Newton, 108

The Monthly Guide to U.S. Publications, 69
Movies, 23
Music, 114

Narrative approach, 108
New York Times Index, 69
Newspapers
  keeping up with events through, 22
  as research tool, 69
  thinking critically about, 118

Observations
  arenas for, 22–23
  explanation of, 22
  questioning your, 25–26
  recording of, 24–25
Op-ed pages, 118
Opinions
  evaluation of, 18–20
  explanation of, 10,11
  influence of attitudes and values on, 37
  informed vs. off-the-top-of-the-head, 15
  newspapers' treatment of, 118
  separation of fact from, 10–11
  testing, 14–15, 73–74
  types of, 9
Overgeneralizations, 88
Oversimplifications, 89

Paragraphs, 122
Peel, Sir Robert, 14
Perception, 83–85
Periodical indexes, 69
Persuasive evidence, 18–19
Persuasive writing
  audience for, 120
  guidelines for, 120–122
Popular culture, 37, 114

Print advertising, 103. See also AdvertisingPrint media, 22
Proof, burden of, 93
Proofreading, 122

Questions
  about observations, 25–26
  of critical thinkers, 47, 48

Radio, keeping up with events through, 23
Reaction errors, 92–94
Reader's Guide to Periodical Literature, 69
Reading
  identifying main idea when, 62–63
  keeping up with events through, 22
  looking for meaning when, 22
  purpose of, 23
  writing summaries following, 63
Reasonableness
  of arguments, 72–74
  of ideas, 6, 24
  of opinions, 15, 73–74
Reflections
  explanation of, 3
  on observations, 24–25
Relationships
  "and," 62
  "but," 62
  "therefore," 63
Rogers, Carl, 15

Selective perception, 84
Slogans, 103
SmithMencius, Roy L., 125
Social Science Index, 69
Springboarding, 47–48
Stereotyping, 88
Stevenson, R. L., 125

Straw man, 93–94
Style, 122
Summaries, 63

Television
  keeping up with events through, 23
  limitations of, 108–109
  uncritical viewing of, 35
Testimonials, 103
"Therefore" relationships, 63
Thinking. See also Critical thinking
  creative, 3–4
  explanation of, 3
  illogical, 5
  instruction in, 5
Thinking errors
  explanation of, 82
  multiplication of, 95
  related to judgment, 87–89
  related to perception, 83–85
  related to reaction, 92–94
Thomas, Dylan, 125
Thoreau, Henry David, 125
Transfer, 103
Truth
  expressed through opinions, 15
  subjective nature of, 6, 37

Values
  evaluation of your, 37
  explanation of, 37
  formation of, 35
  reinforced in magazines, 116
Voice-overs, 103

Ward, C. M., 37
World Almanac, 69
Writing, persuasive, 120–122

About the Author

VINCENT RYAN RUGGIERO is an internationally known writer, lecturer, and consultant whose areas of special interest and expertise are critical and creative thinking, ethics, educational reform, and social criticism.

A pioneer in the movement to make thinking skills instruction an important emphasis at every level of education, he holds the rank of Professor Emeritus, State University of New York at Delhi, and resides in Dunedin, Florida.

Professor Ruggiero's sixteen books include *Beyond Feelings: A Guide to Critical Thinking, Thinking Critically About Ethical Issues, The Art of Thinking, Teaching Thinking Across the Curriculum, A Guide to Thinking Sociologically*, and *Warning: Nonsense Is Destroying America*.

CHAPTER 1 Quiz Answers

1. True.

2. Critical thinking is an important skill. Business and professional success depends on it, as does mental health.

3. Truth is discovered rather than created. The test for whether something is true or false is not whether we believe it. (If it were, then no one could ever be wrong.)

4. The principle of contradiction says that an idea cannot be both true and false at the same time in the same way. This principle motivates us to excellence in critical thinking.

5. a) Briefly note the source of your information.
   b) Treat it as an opinion.
   c) Answer any questions others might ask.

6. It is not profitable to argue about matters of taste. Such matters can't be supported by facts but only by assertion—"That's my view because that's my view."

7. Being entitled to your opinion means having a right to make up your own mind. It does not mean your opinion is always right or that other people must agree with it.

8. Evidence is information employed to support a viewpoint. Examples include statements of reasons, details of past events or incidents, and statistics.

9. Critical thinkers do have convictions. Critical thinking aims at forming convictions. And critical thinkers are willing to re-examine their convictions when the evidence prompts them to do so.

10. The three steps of the comprehensive thinking strategy presented in this chapter are: **Observe,** taking note of what you see, hear, and read. **Record** your observations in a journal, as they occur if possible. **Address relevant, thought-provoking questions** when time permits.

CHAPTER 2 Quiz Answers

1. People are not born with individuality but only with the potential to develop it. What we say or do may express conditioning or unthinking conformity rather than individuality.
2. The first step in becoming an individual is to admit that you've been shaped by your culture.
3. The key to becoming and remaining an individual is deciding to learn how and where you got your habits, attitudes, and values. Then you can decide whether you wish to retain or change them.
4. Attitudes are tendencies to think or act in certain ways, as distinguished from thoughts and actions themselves.
5. Values are principles, standards, or qualities considered worthwhile or desirable.
6. Yes. Values, like attitudes, affect the quality of our thinking.
7. True. Examples of such habits are being alert to what is going on around us, actively seeking out insights, controlling the tendency to leap to conclusions, and thinking before speaking and acting.

8. In addition to possessing self-knowledge, critical thinkers:
   Are honest with themselves.
   Resist manipulation.
   Overcome confusion.
   Ask questions.
   Take the time to produce many ideas.
   Base their judgments on evidence.
   Acknowledge complexity.
   Look for connections between subjects.
   Are intellectually independent.

CHAPTER 3 Quiz Answers

1. No. The term *argument* is used in this book as philosophers use it. To argue in this sense is to present a view about an issue, not to quarrel.
2. True. News stories, for example, have traditionally aimed at informing rather than persuading.
3. An argument is persuasive to critical thinkers when the evidence presented shows the opinion it supports to be more reasonable than competing opinions.
4. The other three steps in evaluating longer arguments are:
   Seeking out competing views and additional evidence.
   Sorting out disagreements.
   Testing the argument for reasonableness.
5. The approach to understanding an argument consists of skimming the book or article and finding the main idea, reading the book or article with the main idea in mind, identifying the evidence offered in support of that idea, and composing a summary.
6. An effective summary is written in your own words, emphasizes key points, and is accurate.

7. Open-ended questions are questions that can't be answered with a simple yes or no. An example is "What do you think about . . . ?" Use these questions when you are interviewing an authority from whom you want to elicit information, including informed opinion.

8. The most important resource available in any library is the library staff.

9. Sort out the authorities' views by making a spreadsheet.

10. False. Inadequate evidence makes an argument unpersuasive but this does not necessarily mean that the opinion at the heart of the argument is mistaken. Other evidence may exist that supports it adequately.

11. The new ways to test opinions for reasonableness are: If the author offers an example, think of counter-examples. Reverse the opinion. Consider the implications of the opinion. Consider the consequences that have occurred or are likely to occur if the idea is put into practice.

CHAPTER 4 Quiz Answers

1. Errors of perception occur before you begin to address a particular problem or issue. They prevent you from being open-minded and reasonable.

2. The definitions follow:"Mine is better" thinking—the notion that your ideas, values, and attitudes are better than other people's merely because they are yours. Selective perception—noticing facts that support your current notions and ignoring facts that challenge those notions. Gullibility—believing everything you are told. Skepticism—doubting everything you are told. Bias toward the majority or minority—unreasonably favoring the arguments of one or the other. Pretending to know—deceiving others and eventually yourself about what you know. Bias for or against change—favoring the new merely because it is new or the established merely because it is established. Either/or thinking—believing that the only supportable positions on an issue are the extreme positions, when in fact more moderate positions may be taken.

3. Errors of judgment occur in the process of sorting out and assessing evidence.

4. The definitions follow. Many examples could be cited for each error.

Double standard—using one standard of judgment for our ideas and those that are compatible with our own, and a much more demanding standard for ideas that disagree with ours.

Irrelevant criterion—criticizing an idea because it doesn't do what it wasn't intended to do.

Overgeneralization—generalization that exceeds your experiences. Stereotyping—overgeneralization hardened into conviction and shared by many people.

Hasty conclusion—a conclusion drawn without sufficient evidence.

Unwarranted assumption—an idea you take for granted without justification.

Failure to make a distinction—ignoring subtle differences between things.

Oversimplification—distorting reality by omitting essential information or ignoring the complexity of the issue.

5. Errors of reaction are defensive responses designed to preserve your self-image and, if possible, provide an excuse for maintaining your view. They occur after you have expressed a view and received a negative reaction from someone.

6. The definitions follow. Many examples could be cited for each error.

Explaining away—dismissing unpleasant facts.

Shifting the burden of proof—avoiding your responsibility to prove your assertions by demanding that others disprove them.

Attacking the person—illogically shifting the focus from the issue being addressed to the personal qualities of the one who disagrees with you.

Straw man—pretending someone has said something that she has not said, and then denouncing her for having said it.

CHAPTER 5 Quiz Answers

1. The terms are defined as follows:

Bandwagon—an appeal to the viewer's urge to conform. ("Everyone is doing it; you should too.")

Glittering generality—the use of words and phrases implying excellence and uniqueness, without being specific about the claim.

Empty comparison—the use of words like *bigger*, *stronger*, and *better* without completing the comparison.

Meaningless slogan—a catch phrase that creates a positive impression and stimulates a favorable association without actually promising anything.

Testimonial—a statement of endorsement of a product or service, usually by a celebrity.

Transfer—the use of a respected object like the American flag, or of an admired celebrity's voice, to prompt the viewer to regard a product favorably.

2. Common in advertising is the appeal to the viewer's desire to be accepted by the crowd and included in their good times. This appeal is often used in beer commercials. Your experience will suggest many other appeals.

3. Print advertising is criticized for deceiving people, being offensive, aggravating the problem of violence against women, and for making children gullible by bombarding them with propaganda. Some examples include portraying smoking as glamorous and suggesting that women are sexual objects.

4. False. In 1986, Minow's judgment of television was essentially the same as in 1961.

5. Television programming, critics claim, underestimates the viewer's intelligence by programming at the lowest common denominator. By keeping young people away from books, it creates mental habits and attitudes that hinder learning. Language skills are negatively affected through the continual use of slang and clichés.

6. Some popular music, critics claim, promotes antisocial attitudes. It also attacks the fundamental values of a democratic society.

7. Critics charge that magazine publishers focus on the sensational, glorify physical health at the expense of intellectual and spiritual well-being, and dwell on projecting a good image rather than on reaching higher personal goals.

*This book was designed and
produced in its entirety on
a Macintosh PowerPC 8100
using Quark XPress 3.1,
Adobe Photoshop 3.15,
Adobe Illustrator 5.0.*

*Basal typeface is Adobe
Garamond. Display typefaces
include Birch, Univers,
and Fragile.*

*The book was printed on
recycled paper via heat-set
web offset lithography.*